DAVE ALLEN

God's Own Comedian

GUS SMITH

ROBERT HALE · LONDON

ISBN 0 7090 4431 3

Robert Hale Limited
Clerkenwell House
Clerkenwell Green
London EC1R 0HT

Photoset in North Wales by
Derek Doyle & Associates, Mold, Clwyd.
Printed in Great Britain by
St Edmundsbury Press, Bury St Edmunds, Suffolk.
Bound by WBC Bookbinders Ltd, Bridgend, Glamorgan.

Contents

Illustrations

Acknowledgements

Dave Allen: comedian, raconteur, television chat-show host, documentary-maker, solo performer and 'straight' actor ... a formidable array of credits for any single entertainer. To ensure a comprehensive picture of this globe-trotting, quintessential Dubliner, I needed the help and co-operation of many people, including his friends and show-business colleagues, and in this respect I was most fortunate. A few people, for reasons I can only respect, wished not to be identified, though their contributions were extremely important to the story.

I am particularly grateful to: Ernest and Gerry Maxin, Lord Lew Grade, Bill Cotton, Ronald Eyre, Peter Whitmore, Donal Donnelly, Bobby Jaye, Virginia Quilligan, Dick Condon, James Green, Michael Barnes, Charles Fitzgerald, Eddie McIlwaine, Joe Kearns, Patrick Dawson, Des Hickey, Bill Whelan, Fintan Faulkner, Nigel Howard, Ted Kenny, Tom McHugh, the late Harry Bailey, Pan Collins, Edward Holland, Philip Key (*Liverpool Daily Post*), and James Downey.

My special thanks to Kevin Kelly, theatre critic, Boston, USA, Clive Barnes, theatre critic, New York, Madelaine Murray, journalist, Sydney, Australia, and the library staffs of RTE (Dublin), Trinity College, Dublin, BBC and ITN (London).

Useful agencies consulted in the course of my research included:

Ireland: *Sunday Independent, Sunday Tribune, Irish Times, Belfast Telegraph, Irish News, Belfast Newsletter*. Britain: *The Times, Daily Mail, Daily Express*, the *Guardian, Daily*

Telegraph, Sunday Express, Sunday Times, Sunday Observer, Mail on Sunday, People, Evening Standard, Liverpool Daily Post, Manchester Evening News, Financial Times. Australia: *Daily Telegraph, Mirror, Sun, Woman's Day.* America: *New York Post, New York Times, New York Daily News, Boston Globe.*

As I see it, most of the people going to heaven will be goody-goodies who spent their lives preparing themselves for the after-life. So they'll be boring people and all the people in hell will be interesting, so that's where I'd prefer to go.

Dave Allen

Introduction

At the Gates of Heaven (and Hell)

And it came to pass that David Tynan O'Mahony went forth from Ireland, and its austere Christianity in the 1950s, to bring mirth to a weary world. Along the way, he was persuaded to change his name to Dave Allen, and in his role of comic crusader became the Billy Graham of show-business. Inspired by biblical parables, God and heaven and hell began to figure increasingly in his funny sermons.

To the dismay of conservatives in the Roman Catholic Church, he was labelled 'God's Own Comedian'; shameful, they protested, as the comedian spent much of his time mocking religion and using it as the butt of his profane humour. The liberal brigade took Allen's side, and, though conceding he was irreverent, swore he was never intentionally blasphemous. The issue appeared in danger of splitting the Church.

None the less, the comedian – sometimes dressed in the robes of the Pope; or the less ornate attire of a priest – continued with his crusade, spreading havoc among the faithful of all creeds. 'I'm an atheist, myself, thank God!' he'd tell them wryly from the pulpit. Yet, he unfailingly sent the congregations away with the words, 'May your God go with you'. It was akin to a church blessing and the more loyal of his vast flock felt the comedian wasn't *that* bad after all. But the conservatives condemned him to hell. Unperturbed, the irreverent Allen used his seductive voice and mischievous smile to win many of them to his side. It was proving a remarkable performance, envied by his colleagues, admired unstintingly by that *other* Lord – Lord Lew Grade.

One fine day in Sydney, Australia, after a particularly successful crusading mission, the comedian was head-lined in a local magazine, 'OUR FATHER, WHO ART IN HEAVEN, WON'T LET DAVE GO TO HELL'. Solemnly, he explained to his flock:

> As I see it, most of the people going to heaven will be goody-goodies who spent their lives preparing themselves for the after-life. So they'll be boring people and all the people in hell will be interesting, so that's where I'd prefer to go. So I thought well, God's fairly quirky anyhow and he'd know I'd prefer hell because I would find heaven more boring. So it makes no difference in my life what I do or say because I'm going to heaven as God has ordained anyway. And that's how I get away with it, you see.

As his popularity grew as a humorous preacher, so did his repertoire of jokes, gags and funny stories. Frank Carson, the ebullient Belfast comic, used to proclaim from the stage, 'It's how I tell them ...' In Allen's case it is particularly true. His story-telling was proving to have a mesmeric effect. He spared no one, Jew nor Gentile, Catholic nor Protestant. By now he was being called a religious agnostic, because he cared about the world's problems, even if he wasn't a regular churchgoer. And although sex, and the bomb, and the human sperm, became the butt of his humour, he continued to spread God's parables and his own notion of heaven and hell. In an absurdly funny way he identified with the holy Bible, and unashamedly he changed the parables around to his own zany ends.

Curiously, not everybody believed him when he said he got more letters when he didn't crack jokes about religion than when he did. Had not religion become an inseparable part of his act? He once sent himself a telegram from the Pope saying, 'I donta minda youa havinga bitta ofa joke on me', and people wrote to congratulate him. And he didn't think that his joke about

Rastus I, the first black Pope bringing new meaning to rhythm in the Catholic Church was racist at all. 'One day there *will* be a black Pope and I hope he's a swinger', he'd reason, 'Do you think I should change the name to Leroy or something?'

He had heaven jokes and hell jokes, but in the early 1980s his favourite was a heaven joke. 'Franco dies and goes to heaven', he'd begin in his typically dead-pan style. 'The Secretary of State needs him urgently so he gets in touch with God, who says, "He isn't here, he's in hell". But God gets through to Satan who says, "Well I'm afraid he's a bit busy at the moment." The annoyed Secretary of State replies, "Can't you pull him away from it. This is urgent." So Satan says, "Well, he's making love to Cleopatra". And the Secretary of State says, "But the punishment, I thought hell was punishment?" And Satan replies, "It is for Cleopatra!" '

People said Allen told jokes about religion because of his repressive upbringing in the narrow Christianity of the Ireland of the 1940s and 50s; that it was his way of getting his own back. Occasionally, he'd remind congregations of his childhood and school-days. He is easily animated. He'd recall his terror as a small boy in a Catholic boarding-school, his body shrinking behind an imaginary door, the only noise the dean of discipline's rubber soles advancing across a linoleum floor. It was only a fragment, but it was still the performance of a master story-teller. Even so, there are differences between the TV image and the real Allen. The sense of mischief is the same, but in the flesh it is coupled with a sober, cutting edge.

He admitted that at some early point in the process which resulted in the creation of humour there was often anger. In his teens in Dublin, it was anger about being 'crammed full' of religious doctrine before he was capable of making his own choices and about the right of people to suppress other people's ideas. He remembered going to a house and seeing a copy of James Joyce's *Ulysses* wrapped in a cover which read 'Holy Bible'. 'The book was a masterpiece by an Irish writer,' he recalled, 'and this was how it had to be kept in Ireland because it was banned.'

As his crusade intensified round the world, so, too, did his concern for the human race. The less whimsical Allen once detected a sense of complacency on the issue of nuclear disarmament in Australia, and he instantly warned his flock, 'I think people here believe they won't be affected, but the reality is that they will, because this country has become a kind of satellite in the US defence system.'

It was this single-minded attitude that made him different from other comics in the business, yet some churchmen still regarded him as a paradox. And when it came to pass that he upset and embarrassed Mrs Mary Whitehouse, and made her complain bitterly to the BBC the churchmen's cynicism seemed justified. As a comic crusader, Allen's name was seldom out of the headlines, but he never once got down on his knees and intoned '*mea culpa, mea maxima culpa*'. He expected his flock to see the funny side of life, and to laugh at its contradictions. As we shall see, his mission reached a critical point in 1990, when he genuinely upset many of his loyal flock who up to then had forgiven him his transgressions. God's Own Comedian had, they felt, let them down. The comedian staunchly defended himself and appealed to his congregations to understand. Apparently some did, others decided in future to tune in to *The Generation Game* or *Wogan*. For the irreverent Allen it was the final indignity.

1 The Home-coming

No one had been able to convince Dave Allen that his home-town had changed, which in one way wasn't surprising since he hadn't lived there for over twenty years. If they had succeeded, he would perhaps have been spared the worry of what to expect.

Autumn 1979, after all, marked his Dublin début as a professional comic, and he was terribly eager to do well. Failure was unthinkable, and he put the thought from his mind as though it was the plague.

He was aware of the chequered history of theatre in Dublin, and it gave him a disquieting sensation. It extended back to 1907, and the riots that erupted at the Abbey Theatre over J.M. Synge's *Playboy of the Western World*, when the audience became enraged at the 'bad language' in the play. Later, in the 1920s, more disturbances arose over Sean O'Casey's *The Plough and the Stars*, and these were again partly due to the language. One Abbey Theatre director, M.J.Dolan, was quoted as saying, 'It is beyond the beyonds'.

How then would Dublin regard Allen's shades of blue humour, his swipes at the Establishment and irreverences? Would his *risqué* jokes send the self-righteous and prudish into paroxysms of rage? At the best of times, more sensitive Dublin people resent smart comedians poking fun at them or at the things they hold dear like religion and tradition; they forgave Jimmy O'Dea, the best-loved of all Dublin funnymen because he 'sent up' the élite classes and institutions, to the delight of the working classes.

There were, too, the begrudgers – as Brendan Behan

had labelled them a decade before – that small coterie of people who resented the success of 'outsiders' like Allen. Most of them could be expected to stay away from his show.

To Allen, it was like stepping into the unknown that autumn of 1979. The thought of performing for the first time before his own people gave him a curious feeling bordering on trepidation. Not that the signs were ominous, but you never could tell when a few hotheads might decide to throw eggs in your direction. However, as a Dubliner, he had more respect for their tolerance and innate sense of humour, and his sole purpose anyway in returning was to make them laugh, in the same way that Myles na Gopaleen (Flann O'Brien) had been making them laugh for years in his column in the *Irish Times*.

He was comforted by the knowledge that no entertainer had ever been lynched in Dublin, or chased out of town by angry mobs. He had to admit, though, that he had chosen a highly unusual moment to return. As Flann O'Brien might say, 'The 'oul place was awash with piety, devotion and humbug after the visit by Pope John Paul II.'

It was scarcely the time, therefore, for a comedian to lampoon Roman Catholicism, or clerics in white collars. Next day, Monday 1 October, the Pope would fly home to Rome, leaving Allen centre stage, and the comedian was not unaware of his responsibility.

It was also Dublin Theatre Festival time, when the city's theatres became a shop-window for plays, musicals and revues. Allen was in good company, for the festival programme included works by Tom Stoppard, Hugh Leonard and Simon Gray and in the casts such names as Sir Michael Redgrave, Ray McAnally and Cyril Cusack. *An Evening with Dave Allen* was attracting a lot of interest; the entertainer's successes had not gone unnoticed, though some theatre-goers wondered whether it would be wise to book tickets for their maiden aunts. Allen had after all a reputation for fancy language, and his *double entendres* could be as outrageous, as they were subtle. His analysis of sex and free love might prove altogether too much for the over-sensitive.

However, Dublin has never been without its amusing paradoxes. A full-frontal nude stage frolic was at that time proving a popular attraction, not only for the younger generation but for their parents. *Yes, We Have No Pyjamas* looked set for a long run at the Oscar Theatre. Michael Colgan, Theatre Festival manager, was forced to remark, 'It's discouraging that some festival productions are not getting the interest they deserve from the public. Is this the way theatre audiences are going?'

When Allen learned later of the popularity of *Yes, We Have No Pyjamas* he was said to be quietly amused, even heartened, and began to wonder if attitudes had actually changed. But how could he be sure until he performed before audiences? Tradition, he knew, died hard in Ireland and he suspected there were still those who might take some offence at his observations on sex and religion. Advance booking for his show was encouraging, and at least he thought, 'I'm not going to be snubbed by my own people.'

To the majority of the Irish, the international entertainer tended to be an enigma. While they admired his undoubted success, they identified with him solely as a TV artist. As a man, they harboured reservations. He had been out of Ireland too long for people to accept him entirely from what they read in PR handouts. They heard the rumours that some of his funny stories were in bad taste, yet they were prepared to laugh at his stunts on television, his zany behaviour and sense of adventure.

It was true, too, that in comedy terms he was proving a controversial figure, his 'run-ins' with television executives getting a good deal of publicity. In 1975 he annoyed a tiny minority of viewers with a sketch that showed the Pope doing a striptease, while in 1977 a *de facto* ban on his shows was put into force by Radio Telefis Eireann (RTE). In the 1960s, the *Ed Sullivan Show* objected to his use of the word 'lavatory' and unsuccessfully urged him to use 'rest room'.

But one of the most widely publicized episodes of his career occurred in Australia in 1971, when he made international headlines. Allen had flown specially from

Heathrow to Sydney to compère a chat-show in which his guests were Peter Cook and Dudley Moore. As the show neared its end, and started to run overtime, the comic called for executive producer John Collins. He then told him to 'go away' and perform an indecent act. At this point, Dudley Moore, who appeared next, said, 'If I'd said that in TV in England, I'd have got five months'.

It was the cue for angry viewers to voice their disapproval. They proceeded to jam Channel 9's switchboard, and newspapers reported that they had received numerous protest calls. Later, through Mr Clyde Packer, joint managing director of the Channel 9 network, Allen said, 'I used the word "masticate" and people can place whatever connotation on it they wish'.

Mr Packer emphasized that Mr Allen was appearing in a 'sophisticated' night show with Peter Cook and Dudley Moore, and since it was produced 'live' it was impossible to edit the offending material from the show. He agreed that the programme contained a number of offensive and irresponsible remarks. 'I am surprised that Dave Allen, as compère, did not exercise more control throughout the programme and particularly in the manner in which he conducted the interview with Peter Cook and Dudley Moore. I would like to take this opportunity to apologize to our viewers and express my sincere regrets on behalf of the station'.

There were also complaints about certain other words used in the interview, as well as the anti-Jewish, anti-Catholic and anti-Protestant jokes. Sir Frank Packer, father of Clyde and chief of TV Corporation, said he thought it was 'a vulgar programme in bad taste'.

To Allen, it was a storm in a teacup and the furore the programme caused annoyed him. He accepted that there were certain risks attached to live shows, depending on who the guests happened to be, but as a chat-show host he had always striven to entertain and provide fun. Both Cook and Moore refused to comment. It was later stated that 650 viewers complained about the remarks on the programme. Allen did not stick around for any more complaints; he left for a trip to London.

Significantly, in 1977, BBC's director-general Sir Charles Curran, revealed what, he said, had been one of his toughest jobs ... defending Dave Allen. As he pointed out in an interview, 'I have defended him on more occasions than I can count, largely on criticisms by my fellow Roman Catholics who find cracks at the Church less enjoyable than I do'.

As he now prepared to come to Dublin to perform his one-man show, Allen had no intention of changing his comedy script, even if it meant offending a few fragile souls. But he would consider including references to Guinness Brewery, the state of Irish sexuality, and perhaps a new look at O'Casey's darlin' Dublin man. He argued that if his show was acceptable to the English, there was no reason he should change it for the Irish. He was not in the business of compromising his art for the sake of a few prudes.

On Sunday afternoon, 1 October 1979, Allen stepped off a plane at Dublin airport, looking tanned and fit. He had come from Bristol, on his own, to a small reception. At the airport to greet him were Michael Colgan, manager of the Dublin Theatre Festival, and a few newspapermen. Allen was candid. Yes, he did know he was rumoured to have deliberately arranged the show around the papal visit, and no, he wasn't going to try and arrange an audience, and he could not say if the previous night's show contained more than the usual number of references to clerical affairs. He told the reporters that his week in Bristol had been a sell out. Later that evening at his hotel he was confronted by a jovial porter who remarked, 'I see you missed Yer Man – Himself'. The comedian smiled and took it on the chin.

Earlier that week in his homily to the thousands in Phoenix Park, Pope John Paul had said, 'Like Saint Patrick I too have heard "the voice of the Irish" calling to me, and so I have come to you, to all of you in Ireland'. The ubiquitous Allen could echo the same sentiments, even if his mission wasn't exactly the same. It was true that Dublin's commercial managements had been trying for a decade to engage the comic for their theatres, but he was either 'abroad' or 'simply too busy'. Now, at last, he had responded, as he joked, to the 'voice of the Irish'.

On Monday, Allen stayed in his hotel most of the day. He took phone calls from friends who wished his show success. He found time to lunch with his brother Peter; they were still very close and had kept in contact. Dublin had changed in the intervening years; for one thing, it had expanded greatly, and the population had grown to almost a million people. The poverty associated with the Sean O'Casey days was long vanished, as were most of the inner city tenements. There was a new prosperity in the air, and the citizens had a lighter step.

At about 6.45, Allen set out for the Gaiety Theatre. He slipped into the building by the stage door and so missed the one-man picket outside the main door of the theatre. James McKenna, a local playwright, was protesting that one performer – Dave Allen – was using the theatre that might better have housed a play. McKenna told reporters that he had nothing against the comedian or his show. It transpired that his own play had been rejected by the festival committee.

Allen, when informed of the picket, made no comment. Inside the theatre, he was greeted by Joe Kearns, the Gaiety manager, who accompanied him to the No. 1 dressing-room. As they chatted for a while, it struck Kearns that the comedian was nervous about the opening night, as though in the dark about what to expect.

'What do you think, Joe?' Allen eventually asked in a deceptively casual voice, proceeding at the same time to uncork a bottle of champagne.

The manager looked across at the comic and wondered what to say. First, he accepted a glass of champagne. 'My favourite drink,' Allen remarked.

'To a successful week,' said Kearns, raising his glass and taking a quick sip. 'What do I think ...? You have nothing to fear.'

Allen smiled for the first time and sipped his champagne.

'Good.'

'I could have sold the theatre out twice over for the show,' Kearns assured him.

'Yeah?'

'That's what they think of you in Dublin, Dave. I'd say that most of them coming in to see you tonight are regular viewers of your TV shows.'

'I'll only have to take your word for it, Joe.'

To Kearns, Allen still appeared nervous, and he suspected that he would remain that way until the curtain rose and he heard the applause. He had known comics and actors who behaved in the same manner, although he had to admit he was surprised in the case of Allen, for he always looked very relaxed on television. Could it be he was expecting a few people in the audience to take exception to his jokes? To Kearns it seemed absurd. In his own view, Dublin had changed, and audiences were no longer easily shocked or outraged. He felt he 'could now present *The Ginger Man* and it wouldn't cause a ripple of protest.'

He had already taken to Allen. Unlike some stars who played the Gaiety, he didn't *act* the star or display arrogance or ego. Nor had he tried to be funny off-stage. He reckoned he should have no trouble with him during the run of the show. Before he left the dressing-room, he reminded Allen that among the former occupants had been Peter Ustinov, Peter O'Toole and Cyril Cusack.

'As a kid, I used to come to panto here,' said the comic. 'I suppose you could say it was our Christmas treat.'

The Gaiety Theatre is more than one hundred years old, and the city's most elegant theatre. On this October evening, it was filled to capacity by 7.50, and there was an expectant buzz in the stalls and grand circle. When the curtain rose at eight o'clock, the audience broke into spontaneous applause, as if eager to give the entertainer a warm Dublin welcome. Allen, in a dark suit, looked a solitary figure on stage, easily recognizable however from his TV image; his shock of dark wavy hair was conspicuous under the lights, also his inscrutable gaze and quizzical smile. He gave the impression of a relaxed performer. Seated on a high stool, he looked like a character out of a Beckett play, waiting perhaps for his Godot. In no time at all, he had the audience in the palm of his hand.

However, it was his voice, soft and seductive, that was his most potent weapon, and it reached out clearly to every corner of the building, ensuring that not a single innuendo or punchline was lost. He seldom raised it above speaking pitch, except when retailing horror stories, and then only for effect. Effortlessly, he painted pictures in words, but what made his story-telling superb was not so much the punchline as the amazing detail. If it was about a drunk, he missed nothing, neither the faltering tone of the man nor his pathetic defiance. The effect on his audience was magnetic.

Joe Kearns watched the performance from a spot at the back of the grand circle. He chuckled to himself at some of the stories, and was relieved that a few of the comic's crude words and inferences did not impel someone to stand up in protest. He knew that years before a comedian would not have got away with it. It was the applause he remembered, loud and spontaneous. To Kearns, it was extraordinary how Allen was able to spin out stories drawn from everyday life and induce people to laugh at them.

At the interval, he joined the comic in his dressing-room and accepted a glass of champagne. He congratulated him on his performance.

'They're a damned good audience out there, Joe,' said Allen.

'It's the best first-night at the Gaiety for a long time, Dave. Did you see one person walk out? ... I didn't.'

Allen wiped the perspiration from his forehead.

'God! I'm only half way through the show yet.'

Kearns said, 'They're saying you're God's own comedian.'

Allen smiled. 'Dammit, I like that ...'

He agreed that the reception was more enthusiastic than he had expected. As he sipped his champagne, he looked more relaxed. He felt good.

'It reminds me of Jimmy O'Dea's great days here,' remarked Kearns. 'D'you know, Dave, they loved his act in Dublin. He was cheeky, he knew his Dublin man.'

There were no empty seats when the show resumed. Again the Gaiety rocked with laughter as Allen sometimes paced the stage and explored life's contradictions. At times, one felt he would be even more at home in a smaller theatre where the audience could study his expressions, for these had become an integral part of his story-telling. The Gaiety seemed too big and spacious for a closer scrutiny of the comic's face and eyes.

In his dressing-room afterwards, he accepted the handshakes of relatives and friends. Success in his home-town was different, he agreed, to success in Bristol or Manchester. A sense of relief as well as pleasure swept over him. Dublin hadn't lost its sense of humour, its love of comedy. It would be next morning before he knew his fate at the hands of the theatre critics. But, as far as he was concerned, the worst was over, the audience had given their verdict.

2   Face of the True Comic

All I can say is that I enjoyed it. Not the sort of thing you'd
bring an elderly nun to, though. A few short years ago he'd
have been railroaded out of Dublin with hardly enough
time for a tarring and feathering. But not now; comely
maidens at the crossroads, where are ye! And on the same
day the Pope left – although if he had seen it himself, may
be that remarkable man might well have had a good belly
laugh or even two.

This was the abiding impression the show made on the
mind of *Irish Times* critic, Niall Fallon, who had managed
to answer succinctly the question Dubliners were asking
themselves that October morning in 1979. And his
answer confirmed that the social and artistic climate had
changed, perhaps even more than Dave Allen cared to
accept.

Earlier in his review of *An Evening with Dave Allen*,
Fallon had told his readers on that morning, 2 October,
that the Pope wasn't a target with the comedian, but that
he was about the only obvious target not shot. 'You might
say,' he added, 'that Allen gets down to the basics; a rapid
round of fire at anuses, vaginas, penises, nose-picking. In
the middle of the Gaiety Theatre last night sat a frozen row
of ageing ladies plainly too embarrassed to walk out; it
would doubtless have completed their reversed opinion of
Allen if he had dropped his pants on stage.'

Considering that most of the papers that morning were
almost taken up with descriptions of the Pope's departure
from Ireland, the *Irish Times*, unlike at least one other
Dublin daily paper, did devote some considerable space to

coverage of the Theatre Festival shows, including the Allen one-man show. Undeniably, the review had been awaited with considerable interest, particularly by some people who forecast that there would be 'walk-outs' at the coarse language. Fallon's next words would be of interest to this minority:

> Nearly everyone liked it. Or pretended to. Allen's technique is complex and smooth, the targets concentrated and worked on. Basically everything is questioned, the set pattern of behaviour, of society, of religion, belief and unbelief; in Allen's worked-out world, the abnormal is the norm.
>
> The trick for the audience is to be lifted on to that single-line track and when that's done, you're away on a hack. He has resisted the habit of many one-man efforts to introduce variety with a song or a dance; the props are a stool, a carpet, a microphone stand that he leans on, twiddles waves and steers throughout. And there's drink of course. He opens with some standard cracks on his supposed heavy drinking, but what he drinks on stage would hardly wet a sparrow.
>
> Gone were the niceties that a telly show demands for its family audience and here in force the exorcized blue jokes told with a rare genuine relish, all served up with the rubberoid mobile face and contorted gesture of the true comic.

Fallon made a point that would not be lost on many first-nighters at the Gaiety Theatre. In his view, Allen's act was perhaps best suited to the cabaret stage. As he put it,

> The comedian over the last few years has deserted temporarily the bread and butter that telly gives him more than once; and his very real pleasure in his own performance and the audience reaction confirms for me one extension of his career – that perhaps he is most at home in a club when a few drinks wash down the jokes better for the audience.

Another question asked that week was: Did one need an eccentric taste to appreciate Allen's humour? It was partly true, for his perception of the human condition was, to say the least, quirky, his view of the world entirely individualistic. To some Dubliners, his humour was not funny, others were captivated by his dead-pan style and subtle delivery. They caught echoes of Jack Benny in him, and that would have pleased Allen; he made no secret of his unstinted admiration for the American comic, who got laughs 'not by attacking, but by suffering in silence'.

'Benny's is a character performance,' critic Kenneth Tynan had remarked, after one of the star's Palladium performances. 'It has a clear and considered attitude towards humanity.' Allen's performance was also steeped in 'character', in so far as he acted out his impressions of popes, drivers, drunks and sailors. With impeccable timing, he knew when exactly to deliver the punchline and make it stick. Unlike Jack Benny and Bob Hope, he preferred to tell a story rather than a one-liner, though on occasions his one-liners could be dead on target and hilariously funny.

The critics, without exception, saw different things in Allen's performance at the Gaiety; none of them panned the show; at least one daily paper had not the space to print a review. Strangely for Dublin, no one commented on the blueness of some of the language, which suggested that the critics' taste, like that of their editors, had changed and the narrow-minded days were over, just as the censorship laws relating to books had been greatly relaxed.

The *Irish Press* decided to send to the Gaiety Theatre a young woman journalist, Ms Cess Cassidy to review the *Evening with Dave Allen*. At that time she was familiar with the theatre scene and could be counted on to make a useful assessment. Under the heading 'ALLEN LACKS TV LUSTRE', she noted:

> Allen takes the accepted aspects and norms of daily life, suspends them, temporarily for examination and points out their ridiculous elements with laconic observation. The formula is almost irresistible. Almost, but not quite. When every ounce of laughter has been squeezed from topics like sex, religion, statistics and media brainwashing, Allen

moves onto the oddities of human behaviour and attitudes to contraception and sex. The material is solid, but not new. The laughs his work receives were genuine, but not helpless.

It's an evening of entertainment, the work of a disciplined professional. But the final feeling one is left with is a vague suspicion that you've seen and heard it before. And without TV aids, Allen's humour on a live stage seemed curiously bare.

Ms Cassidy's reservations seemed valid. Curiously, some people had found the comedian funnier on stage than on television and were more convinced than ever that his true forte was cabaret. The begrudgers complained that his humour pandered to the lowest taste and bordered on vulgarity. But they were in a minority. Allen realized that he could not possibly please everyone. Coming back to perform before his people had been an emotional experience, a challenge, and he believed that he had met it. The response continued to be enthusiastic. There were no walk-outs, and not a single protest by the audience.

Visiting stars to Dublin were invariably invited on the *Late Late Show*, Ireland's most popular television chat-show. Allen accepted an invitation that weekend to be a guest, even though it meant a dash from the theatre at the end of his own show.

There was a rumour abroad that he was banned from Irish broadcasting, but no confirmation of this could be found, nor was Allen himself aware of any such ban. 'We were delighted to have him on the show', recalls Pan Collins, a senior researcher with the *Late Late Show*. 'We anticipated no trouble with him. For years, comedians had been coming on the show and telling jokes without upsetting the applecart. We regarded Dave Allen as a witty talker and funny man.'

To Ms Collins, the *Late Late Show* had done a great service to Irish life by 'opening windows shut for years'. Subjects like sex, religion and women's nighties had been taboo on Irish radio and television until they were discussed frankly on the show. Soon viewers accepted such frankness as the norm. A more liberal air was by now apparent, too, in the corridors of RTE, and broadcasters no longer felt restricted in what they could discuss on the air.

Pan Collins was aware that Allen could be blue, but she wasn't worried. For years, she had followed his career and regarded him in some respects as a comic genius. His perception of comedy had, in her opinion, brought a new dimension to TV comedy programmes. She remembered that in the middle of the 1960s he was offered as a guest to the *Late Late Show* but was turned down. 'Who is Dave Allen?' the show's compère Gay Byrne had asked at a conference, and despite assurances that the comedian had done well in Australia and was now beginning to 'take off' in Britain, Byrne persisted, 'I've never heard of him'. It meant that his début would have to wait.

In the late 1960s, when his name was becoming a household word in British TV, Pan Collins again put him forward as a possible guest on the *Late Late Show*. She had collected a good deal of material on his career, enough to convince Gay Byrne that Allen would be a sparkling guest. Her memo read,

> According to those close to him, Dave Allen is positive (but not bossy), persuasive, alert, alive, totally educated, sensitive, tolerant – and super to work with. He is also unpredictable. For instance, on the last programme on his just over television series, his colleagues thought he might be up to something when he asked for a sledgehammer, but nobody knew that he planned to give away the set, furniture and all.
>
> While Dave himself is unperturbable, the situations in which he has involved himself in his latest show have often been downright dangerous and the director used to go white with nerves – the most dangerous items were the car tank, the parachute jump, the sharpshooter with a .32 rifle (Dave stood in direct line of fire), the revolving board with knives. One night, he actually put a foot through it.
>
> The night he had George Lazenby (the new James Bond) on the show when Lazenby said he was a judo expert, Dave admitted to being a Karate Black Belt and challenged him to a bout – two different media, but it was a hilarious match. I don't know if Dave really is a Karate belt, black or

any other, but he does like to prove that any normal healthy man can do virtually *anything*.

Byrne agreed to have him as guest on the *Late Late* and his appearance was such a big success that some viewers wrote to the show, saying 'we want Dave Allen back again'. For his appearance on this October evening in 1979, Allen would not be asked to perform anything 'dangerous'. His brief was to join the discussion with the *Late Late* panel and tell some funny stories.

In the make-up room, the staff found him chatty and down-to-earth, and he didn't go out of his way to be funny. It was soon evident however that he was in effervescent form and sought to monopolize the show. 'I think Dave wanted to take it over in the nicest possible way', recalls Pan Collins. 'He handed out cigarettes to the audience, joked with them, and could hardly be stopped talking. Considering that he had performed his stage show earlier at the Gaiety Theatre, his energy was amazing. He was a splendid guest, funny and charming.'

It was noticeable that Gay Byrne, a very professional chat-show host, took to the comedian. Despite his lively performance, Allen had not tried to steal the limelight totally from Byrne. 'Gay liked talented people on the show', says Pan Collins. 'He did admire Allen's perceptive humour and natural wit. It was a very Dublin thing.'

In the hospitality room later, Allen talked to Byrne and the members of the show's panel, a few of whom had seen his stage show. It hardly seemed at that moment that the comedian had left Dublin just over twenty years before to try his luck overseas. Yet, he had never forgotten the city, and visited it whenever he could. He was reminded now of those days which he had never quite forgotten. Suddenly, the past rose up before him.

3 'A determined boy'

'David was absolutely devoted to his father', said his mother, Mrs Jean Tynan-O'Mahony. 'I think he could always get things from him the other two boys, Peter and John, couldn't.'

David was born in Dublin on 6 July 1936, but years later would change his name to Dave Allen because his agent thought the name David Tynan O'Mahony was 'unpronounceable'. The O'Mahony family was respectable, and middle class and some of its members were, in the local jargon, 'quite distinguished'. Young David's grandmother was Nora Tynan, who edited the *Freeman's Journal*, and could count on contributors of the stature of W.B.Yeats. His aunt Kathleen Tynan was a noted poet. And he could claim a cousin, Eoin O'Mahony, a barrister by profession who was 'a wandering scholar' and affectionately known as 'The Pope'. White-bearded and mellow-tongued, the soubriquet was given to him at Clongowes College. One day, when asked what he wanted to be, he replied 'The Pope'.

Undoubtedly, it was his father who would have the strongest influence on young David's growing-up. Assistant manager of the *Irish Times*, his background and subsequent careers were interesting for more than one reason. He was said to be the first child born in the British Empire in the twentieth century, for he came into the world a few minutes after midnight on the morning of 1 January 1899 and his mother, Mrs Nora O'Mahony was presented with a big silver cup by the *Queen*, a popular magazine at the time. He had a decided flair for drawing and painting, and a number of different careers seemed open to him.

Gerard John Cullen Tynan O'Mahony was known to his family circle as 'Cullie'; throughout the length and breadth of Ireland he was called simply 'Pussy' O'Mahony. It was claimed that he acquired this friendly nickname in the *Irish Times* office, when he arrived one afternoon wearing a gaily coloured bow tie which instantly struck a colleague as the kind worn by Louis Wain's kittens, and he asked him where he got the 'pussy-cat' tie. The remark was overheard by others in the room and 'Pussy' became O'Mahony's name. Subsequently, whenever he wrote to colleagues, he signed his notes with an effigy of a cat with a huge bow around its neck.

After service in the First World War, he joined the British Civil Service, and later on the commercial staff of the *Daily News*. He became art editor of the *Irish Times* in 1928, and subsequently worked in both the advertising and circulation sides. If his colleagues found him loyal and generous, young David, his son, looked on him as a kind father. 'He was a warm man, a very warm man', he recalls today. 'I remember him as a cuddler, a squeezer, a hugger. He would pick you up and kiss you. He had a moustache, that's an impression, oh and yes, possibly needed a shave.'

The boys' mother ensured that the house was well-kept and clean, and to the boys it was 'a real home', at once warm and cheerful. Both parents were determined to give their children a good education. 'You have a tradition to keep up', Mrs O'Mahony would say, obviously referring to the academic side of the family. David was sent to the Carmelites and settled in like any normal child, but even at that early age he was 'a bit of a prankster' after school hours.

Like other boys of the time in the parish, he became an altar boy at the express wish of his mother. But a rebellious streak compelled him to mimic the concelebrating priest behind his back, to the amusement of his fellow pupils, and to practical jokes such as switching around the Stations of the Cross. 'I was told I could never undo my wickedness for that', he would joke years later. Being healthy, he was fond of vigorous games and was considered good at them. From an early age, he liked animals and soon he had a dog and a goat. The O'Mahonys were a close-knit family and the boys tended to pal together, despite the fact that David was the youngest, and they never wanted for friends.

It was a Dublin of stark contrasts. Wealth and poverty dominated the social scene; the war had brought rationing and increased deprivation and hunger. To David O'Mahony and boys of his age, the cinema was the attraction with westerns very popular. Mrs O'Mahony noticed that her youngest son loved anything to do with the stage. 'I think David knew what he wanted from the age of fifteen', she would say later.

Living in suburban Templeogue meant that the family was removed from the few tenements that besmirched the inner city areas, but Mrs O'Mahony was not unaware of the poverty in the community around her. At that time there was a big annual fair held in Templeogue, and the village children were expected to put on little acts to make a few pennies. Since most of the children were poor, she gave her boys, including young David, strict orders that they were not to go in and take pennies from anyone. On the afternoon of the fair, she was cycling home on her bicycle from the village when she looked across the fields and thought, 'Golly, that looks like my best hat and dress!' She had caught a flash of colour in the long grass, but then it disappeared. She decided to investigate.

To her dismay, she saw that the boys had raided her wardrobe – high-heeled shoes and all – and were putting on a show at the fair. Mrs O'Mahony forgave them because they made more than any of the village children, about seven shillings and sixpence. By now she had come to accept that David was fond of playing pranks and was an inventive and imaginative child, observant and considerate. She noticed how close he was to his father, and how he liked being in his company and talking to him. When his father mimicked someone, the boy's face would light up in admiration at the cleverness of the mimicry.

' "Pussy" could affect any accent at will', recalled a friend. 'He would have made a first-rate comedian; to hear

him sing his cockney lyrics was a treat.' There were others
who felt that his 'personality belonged to the eighteenth
century, in which he would have cut a dashing figure.'

By now he had been appointed manager of the *Irish
Times*, which meant that he had a little less time to devote
to the boys. What worried his wife Jean was his generosity
to 'outsiders'. Friends had warned her that her husband
was an easy touch. He was always helping somebody in
some way, and colleagues knew that for years he had been
'an easy mark' for every amateur and professional touch
in Dublin.

A good mixer, he was welcome at either business or
literary parties, though he was more at home among
journalists and artists and he enjoyed a drink with them.
With his genius for story-telling and mimicry, he was
always in demand.

Just when the O'Mahony family was enjoying a better
life, 'Pussy' was stricken by ill-health and was forced to
retire from work. It was a serious blow to the family. Jean,
his wife, began to worry about the future. On 19 April 1948
came the announcement of his death.

It was the first tragedy in young David O'Mahony's life
and he was shattered. He would miss his father
profoundly. Jean O'Mahony realized that her husband
had died at a critical stage in the children's lives; David
was only twelve and she knew it was going to be a
struggle to rear and educate the boys.

David accompanied his mother and his brothers, Peter
and John, to the family grave in suburban Tallaght for the
burial of their father. It was a big funeral by Dublin
standards, and the Irish Prime Minister, Mr John A. Costello, attended, as well as representatives of various walks
of life. And in the pubs of Dublin they talked about his
pranks, his mimicry and story-telling. The *Irish Times* paid
'Pussy' O'Mahony the warmest tribute: He was a prince of
good fellows, who spent a great part of his short life doing
things for others. Generosity was his besetting sin. Actually, he was born a couple of hundred years too late.

His death brought an unwelcome austerity to the
family. 'After Pat's death things weren't easy for us', said

Jean O'Mahony. It was unfortunately true. Money was scarce, but being the industrious woman she was, she decided to start dress-designing so that she could see her boys through college.

For David in particular it was a new experience. Being a perceptive boy, he realized the new responsibility his mother must shoulder, and he was eager to finish school and get a job. The affection shown by her sons lightened the load for Mrs O'Mahony and tended to make her forget the genteel poverty around her.

Eventually, Peter began work as a junior reporter/ photographer in Drogheda, and John joined Independent Newspapers on the commercial side. And at the age of seventeen, David was taken on to the staff of the same group of newspapers and started work in the circulation department at a weekly wage of twenty-five shillings. It was considered a secure job, almost akin to a post in the Civil Service or Guinness Brewery. His work entailed shifting ledgers from one room to another, also seeing to customers' needs at the front office counter.

There was an air about the building that did not entirely appeal to young David O'Mahony. One was called by one's surname, and the strict management outlook almost ensured that you could never be seen as less than serious. One worked a five-and-a-half day week. To the office staff, it was invariably John O'Mahony who appeared to be the extrovert and humorist. 'He could be witty and good-humoured', recalled a colleague. 'And he made friends very easily. I think that Dave, as he was called then, had cultivated more friends than John outside the office. I never saw Dave smile much in the office.'

Girls in the office found young O'Mahony attractive, but 'hard to get to know'. It struck one colleague, Tom McHugh, that his heart wasn't entirely in his work. 'I felt that he wasn't cut out for commercial life. Perhaps he found it too dull and unimaginative.'

John O'Mahony talked of an ambition to be a comedian and colleagues felt that he was funny enough to make the stage. They were unsure about Dave. 'He has the eyes of a ballet dancer', remarked John Finegan, who was theatre critic of the *Evening Herald*. Others on the commercial side thought that young Allen 'might make an actor'.

Mrs O'Mahony always showed an interest in the company her boys kept, and sometimes invited John and David to bring their friends back to the house. 'I went along one evening with John O'Mahony,' recalled Tom McHugh, 'and she treated us to beans on toast and tea. She was a friendly woman and, to me, looked like the writer Mary Lavin. Her hair was grey and she had a certain nobility about her. When Dave came in he joined us at the table. I could see that he and John respected their mother, and there was obvious affection between them.'

Eventually, John O'Mahony left Independent Newspapers for England, and shortly afterwards David decided to join his brother Peter in Drogheda and find out if he was suited to journalism. The *Drogheda Argus*, with a circulation of 17,000 copies a week, had a good reputation as a progressive provincial paper. Peter O'Mahony was an established reporter/photographer on the paper.

To young David, who was eighteen, the newspaper world afforded more scope than working for five-and-a-half days a week at a desk. However, he was not sure whether it was the right thing for him, but he was prepared to give it a try. He started at ten shillings a week with a promise of more money if he 'made the grade'.

The editor of the *Argus* was Fintan Faulkner, a newspaperman with a particular gift for training young journalists, and at the same time getting the best out of an experienced staff. 'I found young O'Mahony willing and enthusiastic', he recalled. 'I gave him a few obituaries to do and he went about his work diligently. I had no real vacancy in the paper at the time but was prepared to fit him in if he really wanted to stay with us.'

Among the reporters who worked there was Ted Kenny, and he became intrigued by O'Mahony. 'I wasn't sure that he had the temperament to buckle down to the more mundane work, like tedious court-reporting or nightly meetings where good shorthand was required. However, he could be a very entertaining young man. He was a great mimic and was able to invent all kinds of

accents. As a story-teller he was very funny. It struck me
he might be suited to the stage.'

In Drogheda, the good-looking O'Mahony was proving
quite 'a catch' with the young women, and once on an
office outing it was noted by the others that he had a
'crush' on a girl called Nora. She was older than him and
did not seem interested. 'I think Dave was infatuated for a
while with Nora and he expected a better response',
remembers Ted Kenny. 'But he was to be disappointed.'

They were carefree days in the town for the cub
reporter. Some weekends, he slipped back to Dublin to see
his mother. All the time he knew that he had still not
found what he wanted. Whenever his mother asked him if
he wanted to be a journalist, he would hesitate and say, 'I
don't know for sure, mum.' The work wasn't exactly
challenging his brain power, he had to admit. Among the
jobs he had to do was tying up bundles of papers and
getting people of the town to fill in the pre-printed forms
with details of birth, marriages and deaths for the *Argus*.

He had kept in touch with his brother John in England,
and soon he decided to join him. The staff at the *Argus*
were not greatly surprised by his decision to leave. Young
Allen was pleased that his mother agreed to join him soon
in England.

4   A Butlin's Red Coat

In the year 1955, John Tynan O'Mahony was a Butlin's
Red Coat at Skegness holiday camp in Lincolnshire and
suggested to his younger brother that he should try the
life. 'I think you'll love it', he had said. 'It's fun.'

At that time, David was feeling a sense of frustration.
On arrival in London he had hoped to get into
newspapers and applied to a number of them, having
started off with the *Guardian* and *The Times*. Then, as he
liked to recall later, 'I lowered my sights gradually to
weeklies, monthlies, periodicals and even got turned
down by some paper in the Shetlands.' Feeling almost
desperate, he decided to take his brother's advice. At
nineteen, he had time on his hands, but becoming a Red
Coat wasn't as simple as he had reckoned. He was
carefully vetted, and had to satisfy the Butlins people that
physically and mentally he was fit to carry out his duties.
One of the requirements was that 'you were supposed to
smile and look pleasant'.

The Butlin holiday camps were run with military
precision, young O'Mahony was soon to learn. He worked
six days a week, with one day off, and earned under ten
pounds a week; meals were provided as well as
accommodation. John laughed and said that his brother
looked stylish in his white trousers and red coat. The
camps opened in May and closed in the second week of
September.

The job of Red Coat was ideal for anyone with an
ambition to get into show-business. The Red Coats put on
shows for the campers, and the standard of performance
could be high, depending on the calibre of the

entertainers. Strangely, David O'Mahony did not look forward to entertaining the campers. As he said later, 'At first, I hated going on stage, but after a time wild horses wouldn't drag me off. I was getting my first real taste of show-business and I loved it.'

He was performing a double comedy act with Red Coat Al Page, and it went down well with audiences. He continued the double act when they went the following season to Filey holiday camp in Yorkshire. It was there that the O'Mahony brothers met Gerry Maxin, also a Red Coat, and they became friends. 'I found Johnny O'Mahony, as I called him, more outgoing than his brother,' says Maxin, 'but both of them were very sincere and warm-hearted and proud to be Irish. They were well educated and had bright, agile minds. Sometimes at night David would sit in the chalet and read poetry to us. He had a captivating speaking voice and I never tired of listening to him.'

To Maxin, Johnny O'Mahony was a rebel, and a born leader. As he explained, 'Johnny was liable to do anything during his ten-minute variety spot in the camp show. On one occasion, I was amazed when he led the audience of fifteen hundred people out of the hall and around the large swimming pool and then back again to their seats. Only a rebel and a born leader could get away with that. Like his brother David, he was talented and could be a very funny man.'

With 10,000 campers in Filey during peak season, and eighty Red Coats to attend and entertain them, David O'Mahony hadn't much time to himself. He liked the atmosphere in the camp and the discreet *esprit de corps* between the Red Coats. He continued to polish up his double comedy act, and felt he was getting to know how to handle an audience.

'Butlin's was a tremendous training ground for entertainers', recalls Gerry Maxin. 'In time the camps would produce stars like Charlie Drake, Roy Hudd, Des O'Connor and Jimmy Tarbuck.'

The smartly dressed Billy Butlin visited his holiday camps regularly and liked to say, 'When it's wet everywhere else, it's fine in Butlin's'. He was also obsessed about cleanliness. His motto was, 'If the toilets are clean, then the camp is clean'. He carried this further by ensuring that the comedians who entertained the campers were also 'clean', and he ensured they were by banning reference to sex. Mention of politics and religion was also tabooed.

David O'Mahony would say that he and Al Page always observed the rules and got laughs by funny jokes and funny patter. 'If you used any kind of bad language, you were fired', recalls Gerry Maxin. 'Billy Butlin wanted family shows and dare anyone say otherwise.'

During his seasons at Filey, David O'Mahony was encouraged by his brother to make show-business his career. John admired the warmth that his brother projected on stage, the effortless way he got laughs, even when the material was not exceptional. Gerry Maxin also believed that it was David's warm personality that appealed to audiences. He felt that with some luck he could make the professional stage, though like other Red Coats in the camp he agreed that Johnny O'Mahony was often the funnier comic.

Peter Tynan O'Mahony, who by now had taken up a job in the *Irish Times* in Dublin, recalled, 'It was John who provided David with the spark that started him off on his career as comedian and raconteur – and David was the first to admit that. John pushed him along and helped him for some reason – and both David and I have often wondered why – John had never had that spark within himself to push himself along.'

As brothers, all three Tynan O'Mahonys remained close. Red Coats in Filey found that when you made a friend of Johnny, you made a friend of David. After three years with Butlin's, David decided to hand in his red coat and white trousers and try his luck in show-business. His brother stayed on in Filey and Peter O'Mahony believed this was a mistake. As he said,

In my view, David got out of Butlin's just in time while John probably stayed there too long. He was too good at what he did. It burned him up a bit and you know, being

funny from eight in the morning until late at night drains
you. You have to be funny and on the ball until that final
whistle goes that sends all the campers to bed. But John's
day didn't end when the whistle went. He would stay up
talking to the stragglers and his friends at the camp, go to
bed late and then get up early again. You can't do that all
the time every day. It takes something out of you.

Some nights, David O'Mahony stayed up late and told
stories or talked with John. It was reassuring to him that
his brother believed in his talent, for at that time he wasn't
sure how his career would go as a 'pro'. All he knew was
that it would be a long haul to the top if he ever made it.
John never tired of telling him to give it a try.

The Tynan O'Mahony – Al Page comedy double act was
toured around the small clubs and variety halls for a
couple of months. Soon, David decided to go it alone and
parted amicably with Page. On the advice of his agent, he
dropped the Tynan from his name, then found people in
England could not pronounce O'Mahony. After much
soul-searching, he changed the name to Dave Allen
because he realized that his agent had no acts or artists
beginning with 'a' in his alphabetical index, and figured
the change might put him at the top of the list.

He found that audience response to his act was
increasingly good. He began to work his way up through
appearances at strip shows to appearing as a warm-up
and link man for musical acts. He went on a short tour of
South Africa where he met singer Sophie Tucker. She told
him she was so impressed by his comedy flair that she was
recommending him to an agent she knew with several
Australian bookings to fill.

At that time he was appearing on bills with rising pop
stars like Helen Shapiro, and, at their first theatre
performance in 1962, an unknown Liverpool band called
the Beatles. The agent went to see him at the New Theatre,
Oxford and instantly signed him up for an eight-week
Australian engagement in 1963.

Allen said he didn't believe Sophie Tucker when she

predicted he would be a success in Australia. But he was prepared to take a chance. It was a big country and offered some scope.

5   The Australian Dream

As he caught.the first glimpse of Sydney Harbour, and the
spectacular view beyond, eight weeks seemed too short a
time to realize his Australian dream. But that was the
length of his contract for a night club and television tour.

At twenty-six, Dave Allen was a virtual unknown, an
outsider in a show-business scene he reckoned as tough as
anywhere else in the world. Two women at least believed
in him – his mother Mrs Jean Tynan O'Mahony, who now
lived in Surrey in England, and Sophie Tucker whose
advice he had not forgotten, 'Believe in your ability and
don't underestimate the audience.'

Capturing a new audience and making it laugh was the
unenviable task he now faced. He knew he could draw on
his Butlin's experience and his fairly moderate successes
in Britain's grubby clubland, but that was behind him. His
first introduction now made him wince. The engagement
was in the Butlin's camp atmosphere of one of Sydney's
southern suburban hotels.

Allen wondered what he had come to. The lights were
poor, the sound inadequate, the room was unsuitable, and
he himself felt awful. None the less, the audience
response was encouraging enough to suggest that the tour
would not perhaps turn into a nightmare. He had faith in
the universal appeal of his humour, it was drawn from
life's experiences, and already Australians identified in a
good-humoured way with his jokes. When he talked
about the agony of a hangover, they laughed at the punch
line, and he knew he had not taxed their credulity. His
friendly style appealed to them; he told funny stories as
though he was letting them into a secret. It was a new

experience for cabaret-goers.

By the time he had reached Melbourne, Allen felt confident. He was appearing in a comfortable night spot more suited to his style and audience reaction was enthusiastic. As a realist, he felt that cabaret was however limited in scope; it was television that made overnight stars. His opportunity came on BTV 9's *In Melbourne Tonight*, where his humour and chat appealed almost immediately to viewers.

'Dave Allen makes people feel as if he's interested in them', commented one critic. 'To many, many people this is more important than oily charm.'

What pleased TV executives even more was his particular appeal to women viewers, and this soon became evident by the bulky postbag addressed to 'Dave Allen'. He admitted that he liked the Australian people. As he said, 'I like working with Australians. They're very like the Irish. There's a lot of Irishism in them, they're relaxed and they're relaxing to be with. They like you or they don't like you and either way they go the whole way.'

A few weeks later in 1963, on his return to Sydney, came an offer that he could not resist, and he instantly put the thought of returning to England out of his head. He was invited by Channel 9 to host a late-night show on Thursdays, and he jumped at the opportunity. The format especially appealed to his sense of innovation, and it afforded him lots of scope. The show would contain humour, singing, dancing, interviews, stunts, and what were described as 'spontaneous disasters'.

It was a show tailored to his particular talents, indefatigable energy and exuberant spirit. Launching it meant though that the private Dave Allen would have to go public and tell the press about the *real* man behind the comic mask. It was part of the show's hype that the comedian least liked, yet privately he knew he would have to be forthcoming within reason. As host of the new *Tonight* show he could not hope to remain anonymous. At that time he lived modestly in a private hotel, and his tiny apartment bore all the hallmarks of a bachelor pad, or, as one surprised observer put it, 'The room carried the stamp of its occupant's roving restlessness'. The comedian had no flashy status symbols, like a gleaming limousine and fine wardrobe. Actually, he hadn't time to think about such symbols as he was too busy clawing his way up. Eventually, when he did meet the Sydney press he tried to be helpful. They found him amiable, quick-witted, talkative and apt to withdraw from penetrating observation. He talked about his early days in Dublin, and how he later became a Red Coat. He assured them that Butlin's camps were great training grounds and several top professional comics got there training there, including Charlie Drake. When he began to relate stories abut his experience in clubland in England, he mentioned his mother for the first time, and claimed that she once came to a London strip joint to watch him go through his repertoire of jokes and introduce the other 'performers'.

He smiled as he said,

I think she was a bit startled as she sat among the mackintosh brigade looking at her and wondering what sort of kicks she was getting out of it. At the end of the show she looked more anxious than ever and our conversation went something like this, 'Do you have to perform in places like this, son?'
'Yes, mother.'
'Do you see those women on the side of the stage?'
'Yes, mother.'
'You don't look, do you?'
'Oh, no. Of course not, mother.'

He persisted in drawing a veil over his private life. He tried to explain that it was his affair, no one else's. The Sydney press were at once annoyed and puzzled. To the gossip writers, showbiz stars could not expect to have a private life as long as they entertained millions on television. 'My private life isn't interesting', Allen told them. 'I don't want to talk about it. I consider it my own affair.'

When a magazine reporter later quizzed him about his love life, he grinned and told him it was none of his business. 'My business is entertainment', he added. 'I love it. It is tough, insecure, challenging, warming and freezing.'

He made an immediate impact as host of *Tonight*. The show went on the air *live* between 9.30 and 10.30, the only light entertainment of its kind screened in the Sydney area. Up to then the city's viewing public had shown little enthusiasm for chat-shows, but Allen set about changing all that. He decided to live dangerously in the studio; that, he thought, would make them look up and take notice.

'*Tonight* is a success', declared the *Daily Telegraph*.

With Dave Allen as host, the show is pulling in impressive viewer rating. It owes some of its success to the compelling attraction of visiting show-business celebrities – but the appreciative mail of the week is addressed to Mr Allen. The reason for his appeal doesn't spring up and punch hard. He hasn't a dominant personality, but confronts his audience rather humbly and often wins it over by acting the giddy goat rather than by exploding a crack-line of jokes.

To another TV critic, he was 'quick to smile and slow to anger', and was already considered one of Sydney's most personable performers. In the studio his work rate was said to be phenomenal and what appeared effortless to his viewers had often been zealously planned and rehearsed. And he was prepared to take risks, often to the astonishment of viewers sitting at home. By now he was not being described as 'unpredictable television compere' for nothing.

Once, in November 1963, he actually knocked himself unconscious. The accident happened as the 60-minute show was finishing at 10.30 and the credits were on the screen. Allen had been extremely high-spirited, even more than usual. He had kissed a woman pensioner, played the cowbells, plastered announcer Bruce Menzies's face with ice-cream, and had a jug of water poured over him in retaliation.

By now, his audiences had become accustomed to

seeing him involve himself exuberantly in most of the activities of his guests. But there were shrieks of alarm from the onlookers in the studio when he began bouncing haphazardly on the trampoline on which a professional trampolist had just given a demonstration. Suddenly, he bounced out of camera view. Seconds later, a camera momentarily showed him lying inert on the floor.

Two women in the audience fainted. TCN officials gathered up Allen and rushed him to hospital where doctors treated him for injuries to his head and leg, and later allowed him to leave. In the meantime, hundreds of viewers telephoned the television channel and the newspapers to enquire about the entertainer's condition. A station announcer afterwards broke into the succeeding film to tell viewers that Allen had regained consciousness and was all right.

The episode underlined the fact that the chat-show host was prepared to go to extreme lengths to bring excitement to the show. In quieter moments, his fascination with unusual people made entertaining viewing. Before long, the show became compulsive viewing as Allen paraded before the viewers an odd bevy of people. Once, he introduced a man who said he electrocuted his fruit-trees to make them grow. In the middle of a conversation in his sitting-room, he'd get up, throw a switch, and the trees would go 'aargh'.

There was the reformed alcoholic who had found God, and wanted to spread the message by writing 'Eternity' wherever he went. Allen never tried to send up his guests or argue with them. He was prepared to listen to them. 'Usually,' he said, 'there is a simple explanation, like the men who dress up as white knights and go jousting once a year because they think the rest of the year is too full of traffic jams and tax inspectors and mundane matters. People are always talking about the greyness of our society, but if you look carefully around, you can find an incredible amount of joy and sheer fascination.'

To Allen, it was all about individuality. On his show he tended to avoid writers pushing their latest novel or biography, or pop stars on their latest album. That, he reckoned, was the recipe for a dull show. In his view, the viewer wanted to be introduced to individuals with something new to say, and the more eccentric they were the better. As a compère, he knew it was up to him to ensure that *Tonight* never lost its innovative edge or vibrancy.

Incredibly, he had become a celebrity inside six months. Requests from papers and magazines for interviews poured into Channel 9, but he remained cautious about his private life. He said he was prepared to chat about the nature of comedy and humanity itself, but not about his personal affairs. Despite his bizarre antics on *Tonight*, there was still a mystique about him and the gossip-writers felt frustration.

6 The Sydney Affair

In America, Ed Sullivan wanted her to wear trousers on his popular chat-show because, he said, 'Every time you wear a dress we get letters from the Catholics saying you are too sexy.'

For her appearances on Allen's show *Tonight*, Eartha Kitt, the sultry songstress, was asked no such embarrassing question, nor had the Catholics of Sydney taken umbrage when she kissed the darkly handsome host, and wiggled her body as if about to seduce him.

Allen agreed that Miss Kitt made an exciting guest, so exciting in fact that he asked her back again. It was late October 1963, and she had recovered bravely from her marriage break-up to American Bill McDonald, though the affair was, on her own admission, to leave scars for a long time. Her former husband had for a time refused to pay even small amounts of child support for the daughter of their marriage. Miss Kitt had no other option than to plunge into a round of global cabaret engagements, TV appearances and recordings.

Allen made no secret of his admiration of her artistry and unique personality. As he said, 'I think Eartha is one of the finest showmen – if I can use that term – I have seen.' He went along to the opening night of her show and said afterwards that she added 'lustre to the occasion.'

When he invited the husky-voiced vocalist to late-night eating spots in Sydney, it triggered off some wild rumours. They did the town together, held hands in public, and sipped champagne under soft lights. At last, gossip columnists had a field day. He tried to ward them off with excuses: 'It was perfectly natural that during her stay in Australia, Miss Kitt and I should meet.' But the rumours got more persistent. As Miss Kitt stayed in her hotel, the Chevron Hilton, Allen endeavoured to cope with the telephone calls. He admitted he and Miss Kitt were 'going steady', but said that it was absurd to talk about marriage.

'I have no intention of marrying Eartha', he said, unsmilingly. 'The whole thing is embarrassing.'

As the rumours spread, he tended to get more annoyed and seemed to over-react. He was advised by some colleagues to laugh off the whole affair. Allen replied that it wasn't that easy. In Sydney show-business circles they regarded the affair as 'a fleeting flirtation' and reckoned Miss Kitt would forget about it when she returned to Hollywood. It wasn't the first time her name had been linked with screen or TV stars. On her own admission she once had a crush on singer Harry Belafonte. Behind the overwhelmingly sexy image however, she was regarded as thoughtful and shrewd.

In Sydney, she accepted invitations to ladies' luncheons and other public events, seemingly unaware of the rumours. But she confided to a friend that she was not in the habit of reading gossip columns as she had never been 'a showbiz person' and therefore wasn't greatly interested in publicity, although she did have her own public relations person in Hollywood to counter gossip columnists such as Hedda Hopper and Sheila Graham.

Allen accused some gossip columnists of trying to cause trouble, and reiterated that any talk of marriage was rubbish. 'Eartha and I are good friends, nothing more', he asserted. 'We found we were both interested in metaphysical things.' He said they had talked for hours about the writings of Kahlil Gibran, a Syrian-American writer who has published several challenging books.

More cynical Australians weren't altogether convinced. They had never equated the metaphysical with Eartha Kitt.

Now, as she prepared to leave Australia, Allen agreed that most questions about his personal life centred on their romance. He did admit, though, that he intended to see her later in Hollywood, as he hoped to be flying to London by way of Los Angeles, and would drop in to wish her a merry Christmas. He said he would have in his luggage specially bought leatherbound books – rare collector's pieces – on metaphysics, as a gift for Eartha.

Although their affair had been widely publicized, it had not become serious and the pair were not accepted as lovers. A few weeks later Allen flew directly to London for a spot on the Palladium Show and was acclaimed, his drunk scene bringing 'the house down'. The Beatles were on the same bill, but the comedian claimed he got more laughs than the group. 'But that's because they're singers. I still don't know whether they're good singers or not because you can't hear them for all the girls screaming.'

Rave press notices brought quick enquiries from promoters about his availability, and he left Heathrow for America happy in the knowledge that he was suddenly in demand. It was a nice thought, but he had no intention of leaving Australia, not just yet. It had been not only good to him but had given him the chance to learn what television was all about. As he liked to say at the time, 'You can't buy experience. You can't go to the university and learn it. It is like comedy. No one can teach you comedy.'

He had a stop-over in San Francisco and tried to telephone Eartha Kitt. He claimed he couldn't find her address since he lost his bachelor diary, then proceeded to call up agents to no avail. The story didn't sound convincing, nor did his parting remark, 'I hope she isn't mad with me'.

Although she later insisted that she and the *Tonight's* chat-show host remained good friends, it was noticeable that in her autobiography, *I'm Still Here* she made mention only of one TV chat-show host, Ed Sullivan, which to some Australian observers confirmed that her affair with Allen was merely flirtatious. It was the way Allen himself wanted it to be seen, for he valued her friendship. Australia, in fact, had tended to bring out the serious side of the woman. She had compassion for the Aborigines and hadn't been afraid to air her strong views on the Allen show. Later, on visits to Dublin to appear in cabaret, she made no mention of Allen, even *en passant*.

Back in Sydney, he resumed as host of the off-beat *Tonight* show, and assured Channel 9 executives that he had no intention of quitting the show and returning to the UK. His appeal to women viewers continued as his astonishing postbag showed each week. Women wanted to know the type of woman he would like to marry. Would she be Irish or Australian? Others assured him he was 'sexy and charming', and not a few wanted to date him. He told a woman journalist, 'I have never had any trouble getting along with girls.'

It wasn't a boast, it was true. Women found his 'sweet Irish voice' easy on the ear, his charm irresistible. If the adulation amused the chat-show host, he wasn't prepared to be carried away by it. He was too busy inventing new ideas for the show to accept dates from adoring women, though he was seen from time to time to dine with pretty females. For the moment, he was content to stay the most eligible bachelor around, and he sounded almost philosophical about it.

If his television show was often called unpredictable, there was also a certain unpredictability about the way he lived life. Plainly he saw it as an adventure and made the most of it. Early in January 1964, he went to a friend's late-night party where he was introduced to blonde Judith Stott. To Allen, she was good company, vivacious and intelligent, with an infectious smile and lively sense of humour. He was interested and hoped to see her soon again.

Miss Stott was in Sydney in the Peter Shaffer double-play bill, *The Private Ear* and *The Public Eye*. At the age of thirty-one, she was regarded as one of England's leading actresses. Critics had described her as 'perceptive and talented'. In *The Private Ear*, she played a pretty, dim little girl, who, for one brief moment, is reached through ordinary feelings by a lonely and clumsy lad. In the second play, she was the beatnik wife of a middle-aged accountant, who is herself lost and lonely until she strikes up a weird relationship with the private detective her husband put on her tail. The roles underlined the actress's versatility and command of accents.

Inside a few weeks she and Allen became lovers. Typically he was very discreet about the affair. Their backgrounds were different; Miss Stott, Oxford-born, had played more Shakespeare by the age of twenty-four than anything else. It was in a television drama, however, that she became an overnight name. Playing tender and serious love scenes in *A Penny for a Song* had brought her talents to the notice of millions of viewers. Asked if acting had become her entire life at the time, she said thoughtfully, 'Not in a Stanislavsky sort of way.' She was prepared to take some time off for pursuits such as walking in the country and lazing by the sea.

Ten years before, in 1954, the petite Miss Stott had married actor John Burnham, by whom she had one son, Jonathan. The couple had divorced. The divorce in 1963 had made headlines in the papers, mainly because actor Albert Finney was cited as co-respondent and ordered by the court to pay the costs of the undefended suit.

Finney was directing a rehearsal of *The School for Scandal* in Glasgow when he was told the news. With two white handkerchiefs flopping from his wrists to get the atmosphere of the eighteenth-century play, he told a reporter, 'Judith and I are terrific friends. But I'm not going to marry her. I don't intend to marry anyone. Sorry and all that, but I'm not even going to get married.'

The judge exercised discretion in respect of Mr Burnham's admitted adultery. He granted custody of the child to him with care and control to the mother.

Allen was not regarded as an emotional individual, though he was sensitive. After a few weeks of whirlwind romance, he was in love, so was Judith. They saw a lot of each other, and, whenever he could, he called for her at the stage door after performances. Remembering his fleeting romance with Eartha Kitt, close friends took a while to be convinced that he was serious about Judith, but as March approached they saw the pair were inseparable.

As secretive as ever about his private life, Allen had

decided to ask Judith to marry him. She agreed, and he
was thrilled. A few days later he telephoned his mother in
Surrey to let her into the secret, and also gave the good
news to his brothers, Peter and John. The Tynan
O'Mahonys had a habit of sharing good news, and Allen
himself could be most considerate in this respect. The
family remained close and Mrs Jean O'Mahony talked
proudly of them.

Curiously, the gossip columnists had got no hint of the
wedding plans, in fact no journalist was present at the
registry office on that day, 9 March 1964 when Judith Stott
became the comedian's wife. Only a few close friends
attended the ceremony, and the couple planned to
postpone their honeymoon until a later date. Judith Stott
was still committed to the Shaffer double bill, and Allen's
Tonight show was running in tandem.

His agent, John Collins, later refused to help reporters to
find the newly-weds. He was adamant: 'Dave Allen told
me his private life was his own business.' The pressmen
were once again baffled by the attitude of the TV star. But
later that evening they had their revenge when they got
word he was at the Phillip Theatre waiting for his bride,
who was starring in *The Private Ear* and *The Public Eye*.

Allen did not try to evade the reporters and cameramen.
Looking exasperated, he told them, 'All right, I'll talk to
you about it. We wanted only our personal friends to
know. To me marriage is a very serious and solemn thing.
I didn't want it all turned into a publicity circus.'

With that much off his chest, the comedian began to
look more cheerful. He told them that he and Judith had
married under their real names – Judith Mary Burnham
and David Edward Tynan O'Mahony. He admitted he was
very nervous, much worse than doing a *live* show. Then
he revealed, 'We have known each other for about four
months. Judith is going back to England with the play
about the middle of this month and will come back in
July.'

To viewers of his television show, the marriage was the
biggest surprise since the evening when they saw him
knock himself out on a trampoline. Many of them sent the

chat-show host congratulatory messages. In the mean time, the Allens moved into a temporary flat which a friend lent them. They said they hoped to plan a real home soon, with lots of books, lots of warmth, a garden and an Irish wolfhound.

Allen hated the thought of Judith's impending departure for England, where she would be reunited with her son Jonathan. He was aware of the demands of showbiz unions and the risks involved. It made him realize that fame and money were not enough in themselves. He was terribly anxious, as was Judith, to make their marriage work, but already he saw problems ahead.

He had seen show-business marriages flounder when couples were separated for long periods; it was something he wanted to avoid. He could say that he had already found real happiness with Judith who understood him and returned his love. He was prepared to make sacrifices for her, even if it meant dividing his time between Australia and England. Living and working apart, did not seem the recipe for a good married relationship.

Thrice-married Ava Gardner had once summed up her disillusion in the following words, 'I guess you think that mad love can change anything. Well, it can't. You have to have more in common for marriage to work. Fame and money do not promise happiness. They mean nothing without a happy home.' Rex Harrison, married six times, (three of his wives were actresses) had stated, 'The happiest married men I know have a wife to go home to – and not a wife to go home *with*.'

During Judith's stay in England, Allen surprised his colleagues by growing a beard. He decided to grow it after a viewer rang up during his show and dared him to do it. 'I'm very proud of the beard,' he said, 'but it's not my first. I had one about three years ago.' In reality, he was putting on a brave face. Because of Judith's absence he was experiencing a mini-marriage crisis. Home at the flat, he was restless and smoked French cigarettes and uncorked a few beers and admitted he was living in a vacuum. He couldn't wait for his wife to return.

Judith's absence gave him time to ponder his decision to leave Australia. However, he hadn't really begun to make up his mind. As he said, 'This will take an awful lot of thought, and I don't know when the final decision will be made. I'll have to wait to find out what Judith thinks.' Eventually, when she stepped off the plane in Sydney he said it was the second happiest day of his life – the first happiest was the day they got married.

It was a happy reunion. He was anxious to take a short holiday to get away from the crazy world of television. He planned to take Judith and her six-year-old son Jonathan that July weekend to the Barrier Reef, a part of Australia he had yet to see. 'The boy will love it', he assured Judith. He was proud of his stepson. And he told a woman journalist, 'Believe me, being together for only ten days after you're married, and then being separated for almost five months is more than a man can take.'

Soon he would experience again the intense pain of separation. Judith planned to return to England that September for theatre and television work. But before that, they attended together the opening of the Mattara Festival, where he ran into unexpected trouble. Out of the blue, he was accused by Alderman May that he had behaved disgracefully by telling an indecent joke. Later, Allen told the pressmen present, 'I was at the opening of the festival but did not do anything out of line. I am surprised to hear members of the council have taken exception to any of my jokes. I told an Irish joke that I've told a few times before, but I don't regard it as in questionable taste.'

He said he wouldn't dream of telling anything indecent to any audience – let alone a crowd of 20,000 people. His wife Judith was amazed by the fuss. 'I was in the audience and nothing David said offended me. As his wife, I would be the first to feel embarrassment.' Allen threatened legal action to clear his name.

Despite the off-beat nature of *Tonight*, he could say that he had never offended viewers by bad taste. As he explained, 'Never serious trouble. Sometimes a bit of a gripe when I went a bit too far with an ad or something.

But I never really felt any of that. I always had a middleman to act as buffer.'

Once more, Judith's departure made him feel melancholic. In his large but untidy apartment high above Sydney Harbour, he gazed out at the blue water, and had to admit to himself he was lonely. Three months was a long time to be without the woman he loved as no other. Occasionally, he allowed himself to be interviewed by a columnist in the apartment, as if to relieve the boredom, and for one obsessed with guarding his private life, he spoke frankly about his feelings. 'I miss my wife terribly', he said, as he smoked his French cigarettes. 'She's been gone only a few days this time and it seems a lifetime. Each time she goes I get a vacuum inside me. I try to think of something else. But everything and every place reminds me of her. If I go to the airport, I remember my farewell last Wednesday. If I go to Bondi for a swim, I remember the fun we had on the beach.'

Long-distance telephone calls and reassuring letters did not fill the void. All the time, as he sat in the apartment or prepared for his television show in the studio, he knew he must make the decision sooner or later. It began to haunt him. At times, he argued with himself, playing the pros against the cons. Going to England meant a drop in salary, giving up star-billing, and taking second place to his wife's career. Yet, he realized that she could not stay in Australia, partly because her son was attending a school which she considered unwise for him to leave, and partly because there were more openings for her in London and elsewhere.

He was determined not to stand in the way of her career and she would never stand in the way of his, so it meant working out something practical. Work just didn't come to you. You had to go out there where it could be found. His own contract with TCN and NLT would expire at the end of the year and they would want to know his decision.

By early December of that year, 1964, his mind was made up. He would leave Australia after his last show in the middle of the month. The TCN 9 executives let it be known that the star compère was leaving for both working and private reasons. 'He wants to remain overseas for a while and has good reasons for doing so. Dave and the company have mutually enjoyed the association which has extended now over eighteen months.'

Allen was genuinely sorry to be leaving. He admitted that the *Tonight* show had been a wonderful experience for him. He talked warmly of the Sydney public and how their friendly attitude meant such a great deal to him as a performer. A station spokesman said, 'Dave will not be easy to replace. The whimsical Irishman has won an unprecedented audience in our viewing area.'

It was correct. About half a million people tuned in to his show every Thursday night – and most of them stayed with it until it finished, often well after 11 p.m. There was no denying his personal popularity. Hundreds of fans gathered at the airport to see him off. Made up mostly of teenage girls and elderly women, they rushed through the crowd to wish him farewell. But he could only offer one crumb of consolation to the fans, 'I may be back in about a year', he told them sadly. To the accompaniment of three cheers from the crowd, he walked across the tarmac to his plane carrying two large bags. Two small fans who had waited hours to see him rushed after him, one of them managing to jump into his arms and plant a farewell kiss on his cheek.

7   A Flat in Hampstead

After six months, he was happily settled with Judith and stepson Jonathan, aged eight, in a cosy flat overlooking Hampstead Heath. With his wife expecting their first child, and as he gradually approached his Australian earnings that topped about $12,000 annually, he began to feel more secure and less anonymous. He joked, though, about 'too many comedians around the scene and the very real competition'. He had only put one foot in the Promised Land, as he referred to television, but remained decidedly hopeful.

It was like beginning all over again, he had to admit. Luckily, at twenty-nine, he had time on his side, but he was not unaware of his new responsibilities. He was a home lover, and was quite happy sitting in front of the fire when he could. For club and cabaret appearances, he wrote his own material, and swore that he would never run out of jokes.

It helped that he liked the English and got on well with them. Their wonderful ability to laugh at themselves appealed to the comedian in him. And as he never tired of telling journalists, 'My stage personality is an extension of myself, but I'm certainly not the life-and-soul-of-the-party type. I never tell jokes in ordinary life. I'm an Irish drinker – in other words, I'm a talker more than a drinker.'

Determined by the middle of 1965 to make a success of his new career in England, Allen became annoyed by the attitude of Australian correspondents operating in London. Some of the reports they were sending back to Sydney indicated that he was in the doldrums, restless and yearning to return to his once happy hunting ground.

A report, for instance, in the Sydney *Mirror* stated,

> Dave Allen, who only six months ago was the biggest star in Australian television, has failed to break into the big time in Britain. He is working the well-worn circuit of night clubs, hotels and country clubs in the English provinces for less than half the money he was earning in Australia. Since he arrived here he has been able to manage only two TV appearances – neither of which won rave notices. In fact, the English TV writers who write daily reviews, did not mention Allen after either of his appearances on the *Sunday Night at the London Palladium* show.

Allen could be forgiven for thinking that some Australians had not forgiven him for quitting his *Tonight* show, and for turning his back on the people who made him the success he was. He thought it unreasonable and told one Australian correspondent in London, 'I'm not sorry I left Australia. I had gone as far as I could go there. What else could I have done? Show-business is pretty fickle. One day you're at the top of the tree, and next morning you wake up and you've fallen off.'

To other correspondents, he stressed that he had never intended staying in Australia. It was simply a place where he went and worked in for a while. He said he intended going back from time to time to do cabaret and make TV appearances. As he said, 'I enjoy working in clubs because it's more relaxing than television. I can go from one place to another and play it by ear. Doing that television show every week I had to be concentrating on one thing and one thing only.'

To his dismay, the correspondents did not let up on what they described as his 'English crisis'. Mike Gibson, the Sydney's *Telegraph* reporter told his readers that, 'Dave Allen wants to return to Australia with his actress wife and they intend to work together in television as a comedy team'. And the comedian was quoted as saying, 'It's not that I'm not doing well in Britain, in fact I'm inundated with engagements, I want simply to get back to Australia because I want to work permanently with my wife. We have missed each other so much since we got married that now we're together we'd like to stay that way – preferably in Australia.'

Allen's wife paid little heed to the reports and entertained no thoughts about returning to Australia. With her baby due in a few months, she had too much else to think about. Allen himself wasn't homesick for Australia, as a few of the correspondents had reported. He was satisfied that his occasional appearance on *Sunday Night at the Palladium* had brought him to the notice of TV viewers and the feed-back he was getting was certainly heartening.

One of the people who spotted him in cabaret at that time was Bill Cotton, head of variety on BBC Television. He enjoyed his act so much that he jotted Allen's name down in his notebook. The comedian's warmth on stage and his dead-pan way of telling jokes took his fancy. 'I found him a very funny man', he says today, nearly twenty-five years later. 'I liked the way he spun out a story and timed his punchlines. And I thought he would look well on the screen.'

To Cotton, an experienced talent spotter, the comedian was different from the rest of the pack. He wondered how he could employ the Irishman. Perhaps he could find him a spot on the new Val Doonican series which would be screened that autumn.

'I telephoned Val in the Isle of Man where he was playing in summer variety,' says Cotton, 'and explained to him the format for the show and that it might be wise to have a regular comedy spot each week.'

'Who have you in mind?' Doonican asked.

'I think I know just the comedian to fit the bill,' replied Cotton, unable to disguise his enthusiasm. 'The fellow had lots of television experience in Australia and since he came here has not been over-exposed. Did you ever hear the name Dave Allen?'

Doonican had been taken by surprise. Of course he recognized the name.

'Well, what do you think, mate?' Cotton asked.

'Engage him', Doonican said without hesitation.

Prior to his own summer season at the Palace Theatre in the Isle of Man, Doonican had played the La Dolce Vita night club in Newcastle in the north of England. His supporting act was someone new to him; in fact, he had heard that the fellow had not long returned from Australia where he had been successful with his own TV show. When he was eventually introduced to Dave Allen, he found him amiable and assured. Later that evening he stood in the shadows at the back of the room and watched the comedian go through his paces.

'He was really a lovely artist to watch', recalls Doonican. 'And each evening that week I watched his act. I admired the way he told a story, his impeccable timing and the material was funny. We said farewell after the Saturday night show and went our separate ways. I had no doubt in my mind that we were going to see a lot more of Dave in the future.'

After his return from the Isle of Man, the new Doonican series began to take shape. Bill Cotton's idea of using Allen as a regular comedian instead of changing every week was championed by producer Johnny Ammonds, who felt that viewers would in that way get a chance to know him better. The Adam Singers would join Doonican in vocals, and there was a dance routine from the Gojos. The success of the series would be important to Allen and Doonican if they hoped to host shows in the future. Although he had hosted *Tonight* in Sydney, the comedian was not anxious just yet to host a chat-show in Britain, although he admitted that 'overtures had been made'.

'I was delighted to be working with Val Doonican', he said at the time. 'We got on well together from the start. I liked his genuine personality and I think he enjoyed my company. He knew I was determined to pack lots of fun into my brief spot on the show.'

The thirteen-week series opened brightly and quickly made the ratings; even the critics praised the format and commented that 'Dave Allen is a hit on the show'. One critic actually hinted that his spot should be extended to six minutes.

Undeniably, this impact was immediate. Doonican knew that Allen's fans eagerly awaited his spot each week on the show. As he recalled, 'Although only a four-minute spot, it was sufficient time for Dave to win over his audience. There were weeks I remember when that entire allocation of time was devoted to telling one simple joke, a technique he's developed with great skill.'

Like Bill Cotton, the show's experienced producer Johnny Ammonds thought that Allen had achieved an important breakthrough. 'He got maximum exposure and he exploited every second of his time. He worked terribly hard to get his jokes across. It looks deceptively easy but I can tell you comedy is never easy.'

Allen would say, 'TV is a wonderful way to reach millions of people. The funny thing is that the public believe that if you're off the small box you can't be doing well.'

By Christmas of 1965, he had become a television personality, and already Bill Cotton was prepared to pencil in his name for the next Val Doonican series. Allen attributed his success to his experience in Australian television where he had gained such valuable experience.

He found time to do cabaret at London's new nightclub, the Showboat, where once more he explored for the audience some basic themes – life, death, drinking, religion and the English. His portrayal of Irish drinking habits and a semi-articulate drunk, and almost lucid drunk, were hilarious in the telling, and wickedly on the mark.

'In the art of joke-telling, Mr Allen has little to learn,' wrote the *Daily Mirror* critic. By now he was not regarded as a stand-up comic but a story-teller, and a very funny one at that. After a royal gala performance, the Duke of Edinburgh asked to see Allen, who was in the reception line-up on stage with Eamonn Andrews. The comedian swears the conversation went something as follows:

Duke: You are forming a group of your own here?
Allen: It's a secret movement.

Duke: Don't tell anybody I spoke to you – it will be me who will be shot.

By now, the Australian newspaper correspondents in London had almost stopped asking him if he had changed his mind about staying in Britain. One report in the Sydney *Mirror* summed it up for the comedian's fans:

> Fans who have been screaming hopefully for Dave Allen's return to their little silver screens will at least be glad to know he is brightening the lives of English telewatchers. As the comedy act on the *Val Doonican Show*, he is causing a stir among critics. And if he continues to make this kind of impact he is here to stay.

The 1960s were proving good times for Allen. His daughter Jane was born in 1966 and he described her birth as another joyous milestone in his life. 'Judith and I are overwhelmed', he said with his happiest smile of the year. And in July of that year, he scored another remarkable success when, without rehearsal, he stepped in to compère the Blackpool show after Tony Hancock was taken ill.

Earlier in the night, Hancock had come to the Blackpool theatre where the show would be televised and complained of pains. A doctor gave the comic an injection and ordered him to bed. Allen was contacted and instantly agreed to take over the show. Millions of viewers saw him joke and laugh as though he was the resident compère. It was reckoned the 'ad lib performance of the year'.

Allen made no big deal of it. Quizzed afterwards, he said, 'I have a headful of material. I did so much comedy work in Sydney that I could go on joking for hours without drying up.'

The comedian was telling the truth. He continually jotted down notes and observations for jokes, and was blessed with unusual powers of retention. Some papers reported that he got £3,000 for the night's work, but Allen shrugged that off with, 'If I got as much as that I could do an impression of millionaire Paul Getty counting his small change.'

What he got was something as valuable – mass exposure, and he had managed to make the most of it. He had not become the Duke of Edinburgh's favourite funny man for nothing. His line of patter was beginning to take off in a big way, and he was becoming a cult figure. Almost all the Australian newspaper correspondents in town were resigned to the fact that Australia would perhaps only see glimpses of Dave Allen in the future. 'I'm doing tremendously well here just now', he told one correspondent. 'There's no sense in upsetting the apple-cart by leaving.'

8 'This boy has got it'

When TV tycoon Lew Grade asked him to host *Sunday Night at the Palladium*, Allen hesitated and said he did not feel ready for it. 'I'd rather stay a performer', were his words.

Grade understood. That was the autumn of 1966, when the impresario was in search of comic talent, and good comedians were as hard to come by as income-tax rebates. What few viewers knew at the time was that before the cameras started rolling on Sundays, Grade gave up-and-coming comedians a chance to prove themselves in front of Palladium audiences.

But he was to be disappointed by the lack of talent among the 'warm-ups', and had no intention of using any of them in the televised show. Along came Allen who impressed the impresario enough to prompt him to say, 'This boy has got it'. He decided without hesitation to put him in the live show. Even today, nearly twenty-five years on, he can recall, as he draws on his fat cigar, 'Dave Allen was a natural wit with a unique way of telling a joke. Off-camera, I liked him as a person from the beginning. He was amiable and did not try to be funny. He had, what I liked to call, star quality. He has remained a great performer.'

A year later, in 1967, Allen was host of *Sunday Night at the London Palladium* and riding the crest of the wave. Despite the adulation, he was not carried away; he remained curiously sceptical about the 'star overnight' tag. He remembered when he had been supporting comic on the *Val Doonican Show* and how people were saying that he should have his own show, but he'd laugh and say, 'I can do without the headaches'. It wasn't that he disliked the idea of being famous, he didn't want to get too cocky. As he said, 'If it all happens then fine. But if not, I'm not going to break my heart. I can always ring up Billy Butlin and ask for my old job back.'

Such humility was hardly necessary, for with Lew Grade determined to utilize his talents at every opportunity, and Bill Cotton at the BBC predicting that one day soon he would have his own TV series, Allen seemed, at thirty-one, a young comic in a hurry. He now lived with Judith and the children, Jono and Jane in a picturesque two-storey house in Surrey on the Thames. Judith had sacrificed her stage career so that she could devote her time to the home. They were a happy family and Allen was the first to admit that his wife had played her full part in his success since his return from Australia.

He was constantly in the news. It was confirmed that he was to get his own show on Independent Television, *Tonight with Dave Allen*, when he hoped to parade on screen a variety of special guests. He wanted to talk to people in strange professions and with eccentric tastes. 'I was successful in this kind of show in Australia,' he mused, 'but I don't know how the British public will accept it.'

To Allen, it was a challenge, and he loved to tackle anything unusual. As he said, 'You never find out anything about people unless you talk to them. If it strikes me that a guest is talking out of his head, I'll definitely air my views – even if it cuts me up and chops me to pieces.'

News of his new programme made the headlines, mainly because it was to replace the popular *Eamonn Andrews Show* at the late viewing time of 11.05 on Sunday nights. It was one talking Irishman taking over from another. Andrews had had his problems with some rude guests who exploited his 'niceness' as host, and used the show as an ego-tripping exercise. On one occasion, a furious row developed between Peter Cook and Zsa Zsa Gabor and Eamonn looked on embarrassed, unable to control his guests. Allen would hardly let his guests off the hook so easily. He was capable of throwing custard pie in their eyes if they threatened the show. He was not prepared to be drawn into any comparison between Andrews and himself, only to repeat that he hoped he could emulate his Australian success. He good-humouredly summed up by saying that he was anxious to find a man or woman capable of playing the piano with their toes.

He preferred to concentrate now on his show, *Sunday Night at the London Palladium* which continued to command high ratings. To Lew Grade, Allen completely justified his faith in him as host. 'Dave's doing a great job for us', he said. 'He's in the star bracket as TV host.'

Behind the scenes it could be different, as when some artists threw tantrums or threatened to walk out. Once, Allen was called on to act as mediator after the Rolling Stones clashed with the show's director Albert Lock. The Stones were making their first appearance on *Sunday Night at the London Palladium* and refused to join the finale of the show and 'revolve' with the other artists on the moving stage. Two hours before the show was due to begin, the group started the heated argument; Mick Jagger was heard to say to the director, 'Anyone would think that this show is sacred or something. That revolving stage isn't an altar. It's a drag.'

Lock was furious, and stormed back, 'They are insulting me and everything else. Who do the Stones think they are? Every artist that's ever played the Palladium has done it. Why shouldn't they?'

Allen endeavoured to cool the situation in his smooth, persuasive manner by calling on Jagger to see sense and adhere to tradition. It was a true test of his diplomacy. As tempers subsided, he was heard to say, 'The show's got to go on.' It did, and one Fleet Street newspaper headlined the row, 'DAVE SAVES THE SHOW'. The comedian knew it had been a near thing.

1967 was already proving a good year for him. *Variety* predicted that he would be a hit in America, because of his relaxed style and his skill in delivering potentially touchy material, such as religion and sex. 'He does it with such skill that it is never offensive,' the magazine added, 'but to

the contrary highly risible. He sports a deceptively soft
delivery which conceals, but not for long an ultra sharp
and biting wit.'

In June 1967, Allen decided to accept a star night club
engagement in Australia. After his success in Britain, he
was looking forward to renewing friendships. When he
flew into Sydney Airport he looked tired, yet he managed
to grin and say with a smile, 'I like Sydney. It still smells
the same; it still looks the same.'

It was two-and-a-half years since he had hosted TCN's
Tonight show, and he had never met the new compère,
Don Lane. Five hours after arriving in his city motel, he
was introduced to Lane and they instantly hit it off.
'Jeepers,' exclaimed Allen, who is five foot eight, 'he's a
little bigger feller than I am, begorrah.' Lane had been a
nightclub entertainer in Honolulu when he was offered
the *Tonight* job, and within six weeks he had proved
himself.

In Australian eyes, however, Allen remained a legend,
unique in some respects. By now they had even staged the
Dave Allen Trophy Stake at Wentworth Park over 790
yards, and it was noticeable that pressmen continued to
ask him if, and when, he was returning to Australia to
present a new TV show. Even now, a few of them could
not accept that success in Australia was not comparable
with stardom in Britain. Allen did not try to convince them
that as an entertainer he had to move around and accept
new challenges. His success in Britain had obviously been
well-documented in Sydney's newspapers and already
people were asking about his new chat-show for British
Independent Television. The depth of their interest
surprised him, but in another way he found it heartening
that they had not forgotten his contribution to Australian
television. He felt proud of them as a people.

He was looking forward to his two-week engagement at
Chequers Restaurant, where he knew that every second of
his 60-minute spot would be studied closely, if only to see
if he had changed since he left Australia. He could not
depend on nostalgia to carry the night. Late-night diners

in Sydney could be as critical as anywhere else; in cabaret as in everything else, they expected value for money. Next morning, the *Mirror* stated:

> Allen works slowly and it takes the audience about ten minutes to simmer down to his pace. He's rather like a fast bowler: it may be a long time before deliveries, but it's worth the waiting. Mr. Allen has changed from the miscast belly-scratcher to a deft professional rib-tickler. Those who were Allen-fanciers in the past may see his act without apprehension: he is not only good but far, far better. Those who didn't like him should try him now. He's worth the risk.

The *Telegraph* said that people at the night club either loved him or loathed him. The lovers praised his polish, his superb timing, his gentle wisecracks, his easy warm manner. The loathers pointed up the age of much of his material, his failure to project himself in the way a cabaret artist must, his sometimes tedious harping on his Catholicism. The paper's critic summed up:

> As an impartial observer I joined neither school. I recognized his talents, registered his appeal to the broad mass of people, laughed at roughly 30 per cent of his jokes, admired the new twists he had given to old chestnuts – and agreed that he is much better with a battery of TV cameras to pick up his understated mannerisms.
>
> Certainly Allen is much more polished than when he was in Sydney two-and-a-half years ago. His timing, too, has improved greatly. London has also taught him that a comedian must have a gimmick – and his is being Irish. He therefore tells all his jokes with an Irish brogue and devotes most of his material to poking fun at Ireland, its people, its customs (principally wakes and drinking) and its religion.

It was inevitable that parts of his act should be described as 'tasteless' because of his references to Jews, Protestants, Chinese and Catholics, and not a few Irish in Sydney were upset by his 'sending up' of Irish traditions, but these people were in the minority.

The papers agreed that 'Dave Allen is not a bigot' and that made the comedian chuckle. When he read on, he found the logic in the argument reassuring: 'The comedian makes religion and politics and even dying seem funny because he does it with warmth and whimsy. He makes Jews, Protestants and Catholics laugh at themselves because he does it with taste.'

To Australians generally, Allen was by now a slicker entertainer who had no need to rely on slapstick and anything-goes sort of act. It wasn't quite true as viewers discovered when they tuned in to the *Tonight* show on the eve of the comedian's departure from Australia.

Everybody had been hoping that he would be invited on the popular show – and he was on 15 June. Beforehand, an imaginary 'feud' had been built up between Allen, former host of the show, and Don Lane. When the 'feud' was about to be discussed half-way through the show, Allen challenged Lane to a duel with a few slaps of his tie. Then they proceeded to a table containing dozens of custard pies – and Allen had the next laugh.

As Lane stood by in an immaculate suit, Allen climbed into plastic trousers, hat and boots. Then the pie-throwing began. Even the producer who tried to intervene got caught up in the fight. Within seconds Allen and Lane were running around the studio, smearing custard on the faces of technicians, audience and cameras. In the closing stages, the comedian even stopped viewers from watching the 'battle' by smearing custard over the lens of the TV cameras.

To former viewers of *Tonight* nothing had changed, although unsurprisingly they wondered if Allen would try such slapstick on his new show in Britain. At least one commentator believed he would not go so far, but not everyone was prepared to bet. Once more he had lived up – to the description one Australian columnist, Lee Patterson had given him. 'Dave Allen is the whimsical little Irishman with the blood of fairies, banshees and leprechauns coursing through his veins.'

9   Late Night Frivolity

That July 1967, his début as host of *Tonight with Dave Allen* was watched with more than ordinary interest by TV critics. Eamonn Andrews was reckoned a hard act to follow, but the real question was, 'Could Allen repeat his Australian success in Britain?' He had one clear advantage over Andrews – he was a host/comedian, and was already being spoken of as the 'darlin' of the TV masses'.

As an experienced presenter, he knew it would take a little time for the new pieces to fall into place. In chat-show terms he tried to explain the difference between Australia and England. In Australia you did a show every week without a break. In England, you did thirteen weeks at a time, then the show went off for a season, and came back later in the year. That way a show didn't suffer from overexposure, and you didn't run the risk of perhaps repeating ideas of a few months before.

At that time, one of the people in the news was Barbara Castle, and she had become the butt of jokes because of her introduction of the breathalyser which affected pretty well everybody. 'But the fact remains that she is right', Allen joked. 'The drop in the accident figures proves it.' However, on the show he tended to avoid politicians and intellectuals. For his first show, he chose as one of the guests a clairvoyant who was half-way through his interview before he discovered he just wasn't in the mood for 'seeing'.

'He said he could feel certain premonitions about people,' remembered Allen, 'if he could touch a piece of metal belonging to them – a ring or a watch. Billie Jean

King was coming on the programme, so I gave him something of hers, but he was no good – he just froze.'

He proceeded to introduce Miss King rather quickly, for some people had a nervous reaction to the camera. To Allen, the opening show went smoothly enough, with the response of the majority of the guests positive. The critics however were mixed in their verdicts. 'A lively host,' commented one, 'who is likely to get better.' Another thought that 'Mr Allen talked too much.' The most caustic review was Peter Black's, the *Daily Mail* critic:

> Why are these late-night weekend shows so witless? I suspect the answer lies in the selection of the audience. We have Dave Allen quipping to Billie Jean King, 'In tennis the only thing I understand is that love bit', to which the audience clapped furiously. Dave's humour seemed to be supplicating you for heaven's sake, but he could do with stiffer support down the floor.

Sunday night viewers had become accustomed to what some critics called 'frivolity'. Chat was considered cheap and viewers had come to expect the unpredictable from celebrity guests, even if this meant vulgarity. Allen stressed that his show was about people, and in subsequent weeks he included a man who could eat dozens of eggs in a minute, an elderly inventor who'd built an aeroplane and a team of competitors in the Cumberland face-pulling championship, whose main problem was in deciding whether or not to take their teeth out before they went on camera.

Despite the mixed reviews, the show quickly jumped into the top ten ratings and stayed there. Allen was confident about its staying power. Viewers liked the unusual, and in their letters encouraged him to discover more 'eccentrics'. For them, it was the show's main attraction, though Allen's own fan mail had increased week by week. By now *Tonight with Dave Allen* bore little resemblance to the *Eamonn Andrews Show*; it was more inventive and more entertaining and guests were seldom, if ever, patronized, or kept on a tight rein.

The news that his wife Judith was pregnant and the baby was due in the spring of 1968 excited Allen no end. The prospect of an 'heir to the Allen throne' tickled his fancy. He was voted British Television Personality of the Year, the first major award to come his way. As usual, he tended to be philosophical. 'Awards, a whole stack of them, still can't change your emotions, or calm your nerves.' He was referring to the twelve million viewers who had watched *Tonight with Dave Allen* and that, he admitted, was a bit frightening.

Early in May he was elated with the birth of a baby boy, his first son. He was christened Edward James Tynan O'Mahony, thus maintaining the Tynan O'Mahony link. Shortly after the celebrations he had to hasten to Sydney to begin a five-week tour of nightclubs and take in TV appearances. Reporters in Sydney found that success had not changed the comedian. 'He is still the same friendly, easy-going character who left here four years ago', commented one morning paper.

Although he made a return visit in 1967, it was clear that Australians now regarded him as a big star in British show-business terms. They were not surprised to hear him say that he would like to try something new, perhaps movies. As he explained, 'You spend a lot of time developing and you have to watch for the right vehicle – otherwise you risk losing what you have got.'

To Australians, the flamboyant Irish comedian was never lost for words and was prepared to talk about anything from icebergs to French farmers. When he was asked by one reporter if he was overexploiting the fact that he was Irish, he quickly replied, 'Humour is nothing else but elaboration really, blown up versions of true life. Irish humour consists of five basic themes – life, death, religion, drinking and the English. No, I don't think that would be a fair criticism.'

In Sydney, he was always welcome on his old programme, *Tonight*, and on this occasion entered unannounced and crashed a custard pie on the producer's face. The audience roared with laughter. He then casually joined the new host, John Laws, who was interviewing

James Mason. After swapping a few jokes and affectionately pulling a few noses, he took his leave.

He was enjoying the tour. Crowds enjoyed his sixty-minute spot in Chequers Restaurant and other Sydney night clubs and he found time to dine with his brother John who was doing well in Australian television, though never likely to emulate his younger brother. They had plenty to talk about – their Red Coat days at Filey holiday camp and their own careers. As brothers, they had remained very close. John revelled in Dave's success and knew that he could take part of the credit for he had never ceased to encourage him to go professional.

By now Allen himself was becoming restless and longed to see Judith and the children again. He was able to joke about his baby son, 'We've got a real regal future planned for him, even though he's a commoner'.

He was going back to a new late-night show which would be screened on Saturdays. Early that September, however, he ran into controversy when ITV decided to switch the *Dave Allen Show* to early evening to take over from *Frost on Saturday*, which would be relegated out of prime viewing time to 10.55 in the London and Northern regions, and recorded for showing the following Mondays in the Midlands and Yorkshire. The 'new look' schedule included Allen's show networked over most of the country at 7.10 on Saturdays.

The ATV boss Lew Grade explained that the decision to move the David Frost show to Mondays for Midlands audiences was due to viewers' reactions. He denied that he was responsible for the switch. 'Frost is a very talented performer,' said the TV tycoon, 'but whether it is right for him to appear three times in one week is for the public to judge. And the public is not slow to make its views and opinions known.'

Privately, it was known that Grade felt Allen's greater pulling power would boost the Saturday early evening figures, and in the corridors of power he made no secret of his feeling. The tabloids took up the story with headlines like, 'DAVE ALLEN FREEZES OUT FROST', and 'FROST

GETS THE COLD SHOULDER'. However, neither Allen nor Frost encouraged a 'personality battle', and were careful to avoid mention of names. Frost, a major shareholder in the new London Weekend Television Company, was one of the highest-paid personalities in British television, though it could be said that he was not universally popular.

Allen's swift reaction to the proposed switch took Lew Grade and ATV chiefs by complete surprise. They had not anticipated trouble from the popular comedian, and, when it came, they hardly knew how to react. Plainly, Allen wasn't having any change foisted on him and notified ATV to this effect. He explained that his whole show was designed for late-night audiences and was simply not aimed at people who would be watching earlier in the evening.

'I have prepared a relaxed programme for viewers who want to put their feet up after a long day', he said. His stand shocked ITV planners who believed they had solved their weekend problems. It also underlined Allen's utter belief in his own ability as comedian and chat-show host. Although he got on extremely well with Lew Grade, and was the first to recognize the power he wielded in TV and show-business generally, he was not prepared to accept change.

To Allen, it wasn't a question of pride or star status, but principle. David Frost wasn't his concern. He was under contract to ATV for a late-night show and wasn't going to budge. All ATV would say was that they were 'sympathetic' and made no further comment.

When leading Irish showbiz columnist, Des Hickey talked to the comedian in London that October, he asked him frankly if he would have made the same stand a year before when his star was in the ascendant. 'Yes, I think I would', came the calm reply, and Hickey had no reason to doubt it.

None the less, he had to admit that Allen's action had caused surprise in Dublin. Allen read his thoughts, and remarked, 'There was no row. I had signed a contract to do a late-night show, and late night to me means after ten o'clock, not seven. I simply gave them my point of view and they were very understanding. I mean, when they looked into my contract they found that it was just as I had told them. They hadn't known. The talk of a row was more a suggestion than a statement.'

Hickey had worked in Independent Newspapers in Dublin with David Tynan O'Mahony, as Allen was known then, and followed his progress with genuine interest. His rise to fame had not altogether surprised him. In recent times he had enjoyed his programme and the personalities he had presented. 'I also admired Dave's stunts', he recalled. 'His jumping by parachute, battling with a police dog, being pummelled by a masseuse and chasing performing fleas. He was doing the sort of thing that Eamonn Andrews would never have attempted. As a TV host, he was an inventor.'

It was true. The previous week, Allen had tried some Russian dancing and challenged the British 'conker' champion to a contest. Between these items he sandwiched a straight-faced interview with an intense American film director, John Cassavetes. The versatility of the man baffled Hickey, who was now prompted to ask, 'How do you do it, Dave?'

Allen answered in a soft Irish brogue, 'No bother. I don't find it unusual to introduce serious people on the show, nor do the audience. For me it just means a change of pace.'

'But your stunts – aren't you afraid you'll hurt yourself?'

'Up 'til now my only injury has been a shinbone when I walked into the desk on the studio floor.'

Hickey found that by now Allen was 'Dave' to British audiences and gossip writers, just as 'Eamonn' meant only one TV personality. When their discussion came round to movies, he found that the comedian was interested, but refused to be drawn. All he would say was, 'It will probably be an American movie since most British movies these days are American.'

It had puzzled Hickey that he had not come back to Dublin on a regular basis to play cabaret or do a solo show. Allen explained that he had intended going back months before, but a serious outbreak of foot-and-mouth disease there prevented him. Instead, he stayed in London and made a television commercial for the Irish government asking the Irish in Britain not to go home for Christmas.

'In Ireland, they only know you as a television performer', Hickey reminded the star.

'I suppose that's true. I know they want me in Dublin. My agent gets calls to find out if I'm free to go. Yes, I intend to do a stage show there when I'm free to do so.'

Hickey felt he meant it.

10 'Thinking is my hobby'

Tom Sloan, BBC's head of light entertainment, had come to admire Allen's comedy gifts and cool façade enormously, and engaged him for a new series. One day in 1969, he asked Ernest Maxin if he would like to direct the comedian. The highly rated producer replied unhesitatingly, 'I've been trying to do a Dave Allen comedy series for years.'

''Twill be a TV spectacular,' said Sloan, 'with British and American guest stars.'

Maxin was enthusiastic. TV spectaculars were regarded as his forte; he had successfully produced Harry Secombe, Max Bygraves, Petula Clark and Tommy Steele, and years before had fallen in love with Hollywood musicals – Fred Astaire and Ginger Rogers spectaculars enthralled him. He had once tried, though, to make Eamonn Andrews sing in a BBC show, and it proved disastrous. 'If Eamonn ever sings again, I'll divorce him', Grainne Andrews had warned.

Maxin first met Allen when he was invited by his brother Gerry Maxin to attend a variety show at the Finsbury Park Theatre in the early 1960s. Gerry, who was by then a theatrical agent, had worked as a Red Coat with Allen in Filey holiday camp in Yorkshire and knew him then as David Tynan O'Mahony.

'You must come and see this Dave Allen', he had told Ernest. 'I think he has really got something.'

Ernest remembers the occasion and the almost instant impact the young comedian made on him.

> Dave Allen did not explode on stage like Ken Dodd, or come on smoking a cigar; he walked on casually as if about

Allen's smile of success in Sydney, Australia, where he got the opportunity he wanted

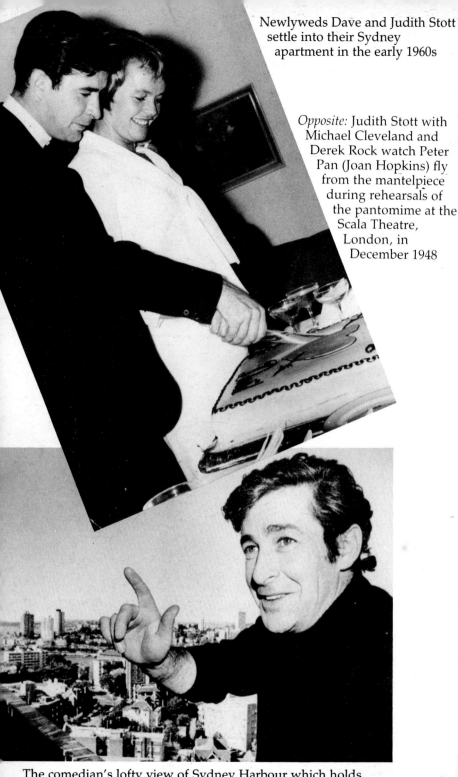

Newlyweds Dave and Judith Stott settle into their Sydney apartment in the early 1960s

Opposite: Judith Stott with Michael Cleveland and Derek Rock watch Peter Pan (Joan Hopkins) fly from the mantelpiece during rehearsals of the pantomime at the Scala Theatre, London, in December 1948

The comedian's lofty view of Sydney Harbour which holds sweet memories for him

Television chat-show host Allen
pictured with one of his guests,
Olivia Newton-John,
in Sydney

Eartha Kitt had a brief
flirtation with the
comedian after her
appearance on his
TV chat show, but
Allen denied
any hint of
marriage

Success on the *Val Doonican Show* made Allen a star name in British television

Lord Lew Grade was among the first to recognize Allen's comic genius

The faces of the comedian reflect the mood of his stage act, which is performed with the minimum of props

Allen prepares to deliver the punch-line

Putting a shine on his act . . . Allen stops *en route* to the Talk of the Town restaurant in London where his cabaret act was acclaimed

Ernest Maxin found working with the comedian in TV spectaculars most rewarding . . .

to make an announcement to the audience. He wore no outlandish costume or false nose like a clown, only a dark suit, and during his act either sat on a high stool or stood on stage as he told his gags and stories. I found him funny, sometimes hilarious, but it was his timing that really impressed me. It was so good that it suggested an older and more experienced comedian. Furthermore, I was taken by his stage presence and smooth Irish charm; he kind of disarmed you before he opened his mouth and to me that is star quality. He was a natural comic and during the evening his comedy seemed effortless.

After the show, the brothers proceeded backstage. 'You must meet Dave', remarked Gerry Maxin. 'He's easy to talk to.' To Ernest Maxin, the young comedian was friendly and talkative. 'You were great', he told him. 'I'd like to work with you one day on a TV series.'

Allen, who was removing his make-up, grinned, 'I'd love to. I'm looking for work.'

'You shouldn't have to, with your line of comedy.'

Allen essayed a smile. 'Keep me in mind.'

Since childhood, Maxin had loved comedy. Born in the East End of London, where poverty was rife, the only entertainment he and his brother and sister could get out of life was trying to keep each other happy. As a kid, he was always inventing something funny to cheer up his parents who were stall holders at the local market. He went on to become a piano-player, dancer and choreographer. His apprenticeship in the theatre led him to the world of television where, he was like 'a hungry man let loose on a feast'.

The new series consisted of hour-long shows comprising singing, dancing, comedy sketches and Allen's own solo spot before the end. It provided him with ample scope to exploit his versatility and art of story-telling. To Maxin, he was an actor/comedian with a style more reminiscent of Jack Benny than Arthur Askey, and he was not surprised to hear Allen say one day, 'Benny's my favourite funny man.' At that time, he was also the director's. Maxin had produced fourteen Benny shows for the BBC, the first British director to work with the great American comedian.

He soon discovered that the *Dave Allen Show* was taking up all his time. Like Benny, Allen was a perfectionist who was not satisfied unless a scene worked smoothly from beginning to end. They were on the same wavelength, and while the comedian always accepted direction, he would occasionally come back and say, 'Wouldn't it be better if we approached the scene from this end, Ernest?'

'Yes, that's great, Dave', Maxin would reply, as they reworked a sketch. Suddenly he would remark, 'Wonderful … no, wait a minute, Dave. If we do it that way the impact is not the same.' They bounced off each other, tossing around ideas. As Maxin recalled, 'All the sketches started from Dave's brain, and even if I came up with one or two good ideas, he was the main inventor.'

One of the ideas scripted by Maxin provided the comedian with a real highlight. It was a finale scene, set in a large store – a kind of departmental store of show-business – with each floor depicting the different layers in the business – variety, films, cabaret, comedy. Allen portrayed Chaplin, Valentino, Jimmy Durante and others without donning costumes, but by accents and expressions. To Maxin, the scene emphasized the comedian's perception and versatility.

As the ratings rose, Allen realized that success at the BBC was important; he had scaled a new peak of popularity with viewers. Another comic highlight was undeniably the sketch billed as the Buckingham Palace 'episode'. The central characters were a palace sentry (Lionel Jeffries) in red uniform and big busby hat, pictured standing motionless at the iron gates, and beside him, an obviously inebriated tourist (Allen) in sports jacket and trousers holding in one hand a newspaper with chips.

The studio audience roar with laughter as Allen tries with drunken bravado to make the sentry respond, first by slowly stuffing a chip up his nostrils, then slowly turning it round, but the sentry does not move or blink. As the tourist proceeds to repeat the dose, Maxin thinks that Jeffries must relent or at least bite his bottom lip. As the audience laugh uncontrollably, the sentry stands staring ahead, seemingly oblivious of the tourist's carry-on. Eventually, Maxin thinks, 'Jeffries must go now, he can't keep up the façade any longer.' But the sentry neither smiles nor moves and the drunken tourist admits his defeat.

At the rehearsal, Maxin thinks it is the funniest sketch so far of the series. He compliments Lionel Jeffries for his 'incredible showing', then turns to Allen and remarks, 'Don't you think it's a wonderful scene, Dave?' To his surprise, the comedian replies, 'I don't know, Ernest. I'm not really satisfied.'

'Didn't you hear the audience go hysterical?'

'No, not really. I think I should have done it better.'

It was this professional attitude that so impressed Maxin as to make him compare the comedian with the star Americans he had directed; it was the same kind of professionalism, a feeling of never being truly satisfied. Later, in another sketch in the series he asked Allen to do a dance routine with Matt Monroe and actor Edward Woodward, but the comedian was unhappy about the idea.

'No, Ernest, you'll never get me to dance like Gene Kelly.'

'Yes, you *will* dance, Dave.'

'I tell you it's not for me, Ernest.'

The director persuaded him to try the dance and he loved every moment of the routine. 'At the beginning, Dave hadn't dancing feet, but at the end he had', Maxin recalls.

He felt, as the weeks passed, that he had come to know the comedian as both actor and friend. He decided, however, to keep the relationship on a working basis, declining to visit Allen's home in Hampstead. 'I feel when you are working with someone, particularly working hard,' he reasoned, 'you become emotionally involved, so it's better not to socialize together to any great extent. This leaves you fresh to renew work next morning; even over lunch we avoided talk about the show. Once you start taking the business into your private life you lose a certain professionalism, for you start to look at a thing in a personal way.'

He found American response to the *Dave Allen Show* very encouraging. Once, when he rang Ed Nelson, one of the stars of *Peyton Place*, and told him he wanted him on the show, Nelson said, 'I'd love to come over'. Like Benny, Allen was amiable off-camera with the same dry humour. In Maxin's view, the American stars loved working with the Irish comic and regarded the experience as 'a kind of dream'.

Before the series finished, he discussed future projects with the comedian. 'I used to tell Dave that I'd love to do a dramatic thriller with him, but I got the impression that he thought, "What if I make a hash of it?" He was cautious about new things, yet to me he never lacked confidence, though he did want a project to be ideal for him before he took it seriously.'

After working closely with him for three months on the series, Maxin was convinced that Allen had the potential to be a romantic movie star. Most of the mail for the *Dave Allen Show* came from women who found his charm irresistible. To the director, there was something of the Cary Grant about Allen's urbane image and he wondered why he hadn't thought of concentrating on movies. Once, he talked to him about the subject, but all the comedian would say was, 'I'd love to do it, Ernest.' His answer lacked conviction, as if his priorities were TV and cabaret. In Maxin's eyes, it was a shame, for Allen's charm, good looks and obvious acting ability would be definite assets in the movie world.

In fact, the comedian *was* thinking about a career in movies, even if Hollywood seemed a very long distance away. It was at that time one of the reasons why he had decided to travel to Australia. He had been offered a character role in a new movie to be shot on location in Sydney and elsewhere. When he arrived at the airport, he said he hadn't brought Judith and the children with him because the movie's budget was too small. He still wasn't sure what role he was playing. As he explained, 'They've changed it since I saw the script. But I expect to be here for some weeks. It's my first movie and very likely my last, especially after I get among the grapes in the Hunter Valley.'

When he was quizzed about the size of the cheque he expected from the movie, he instantly put up his guard and ducked the question. 'I'm a sly, cheeky swine and I never talk about money. It's none of your business anyway.' While in Australia he assured reporters that he would not consider any offers for a TV show as his career was now in Britain and there were plans for a new series.

Allen was the last overseas star to sign for the movie, which began as *Squeeze a Flower, Squeeze a Grape*, was changed to *Squeezed Grape* and ended up *Squeeze a Flower*. The production was reputed to be the first important move towards establishing an Australian movie industry, although part of the budget for the *Squeeze a Flower* came from an American source. Among the stars already signed up were Walter Chiari and Jack Albertson. The plot, by no means subtle, centres round an Italian monastery where only the monks know the secret formula for making the liqueur Benedictine. Brother George (Walter Chiari) disgusted at the small percentage the monastery makes from the retail price, tries to persuade the abbot to make their business more commercial. Failing in his endeavour, he leaves the monastery and goes to Australia to produce wine with a second generation Italian family, headed by Jack Albertson and his son-in-law Dave Allen.

To Allen, the plot had a neat twist and he described the movie as 'a light comedy'. He stressed that his wasn't exactly a starring role and said it was too early to talk about his future plans in movies. 'It's in the lap of the gods', he remarked, obviously eager now to get among the grapes in Hunter Valley.

Squeeze a Flower went on general release in Britain early in 1970 and enjoyed moderate success for its makers, the Australian company Group W. Chiari and Albertson stole the honours, but Allen's performance did not go completely unnoticed by the film critics.

11   Bill Cotton's Decision

In a tiny, scruffy office on the fourth floor of BBC's Television Centre, Allen sat smoking French cigarettes and drinking tea as his scriptwriters Austin Steele and Peter Vincent kicked over ideas for the new six-part series *Dave Allen at Large*. It was August 1970, five months before the series was due to be screened.

It was Bill Cotton, head of variety, who had handed the new BBC2 contract to the comedian. He had tremendous faith in his ability and reckoned he should be given more rein. Cotton chose Peter Whitmore to produce and direct the new series, convinced that with his innate flair for comedy he would quickly establish a successful rapport with the comedian.

Whitmore, a genial six-footer, had invited Allen to his office for long talks about the series, intent on getting to know him. 'I found him very pleasant,' he recalls, 'and a quiet and gentle man. But he knew exactly what he wanted. My job was to create the right atmosphere for his talent and to ensure that it was *him* that was getting across to viewers. You would never think talking to him that he was one of the country's most outstanding funny men.'

To the director, five months seemed a long time to devote to the series. However, as the weeks slipped by and sketches took shape, he began to appreciate how much was involved in the making of a big TV series. Being asked to direct it was an important step for him, and he was keen to reward Bill Cotton's faith in him. Ever since Whitmore had directed *Crackerjack* for Eamonn Andrews, he had come to love television. He had joined the BBC in 1941 and worked his way up from sound radio to TV floor manager, where he worked with David Nixon and Michael Bentine. Later, he produced a light entertainment show for Terry Scott and June Whitfield. Now the *Dave Allen at Large* posed an interesting new challenge as they were about to try out a new technique, which meant that sketches would no longer be done before a studio audience but prerecorded on film. The idea was that when the audience arrived in the studio all they saw was Allen sitting on a stool about to tell gags and introduce the recorded sketches during the show. Bill Cotton worried about this novel approach as he feared it would not appeal to audiences. As he said, 'People want to feel the excitement of cameramen dashing about and changing scenery, not to be introduced to the finished product'.

He advised Whitmore to do six of the sketches in front of the audience, but it was too late and contrary to the whole planning of the thing. Furthermore, Allen found the new technique stimulating. Whitmore conveniently forgot Cotton's advice, and the audience did not seem disappointed. *Dave Allen at Large* had a running time of fifty minutes, and about twenty-five minutes was taken up with the comedian perched on a high stool telling jokes; nearly twenty minutes was devoted to sketches which the audience watched from screens around the studio. Some of the quickies ran for only thirty seconds.

When not prerecording sketches, the scriptwriters worked away in their tiny office on the fourth floor of the TV Centre. Peter Whitmore and the production team had already put word around to the rest of the writing fraternity that they were in the market for sketches for the Allen show. Soon lots of old sketches arrived in the office and were discussed by Allen, Whitmore and the scriptwriters. After reading a sketch, the comedian might say, 'Yes, yes', or 'No, thank you'. Once he decided that sketches were funny he began to dress them up and record them on film. Sometimes he changed around a script, but was always careful to acknowledge the writer in the credits. So anxious was he to get the series right, that he cut out all his other engagements for five months. Watching him at work, Whitmore was astonished by his attention to detail. 'He never once spared himself,' said the producer.

He found that the comedian liked the idea of filming Robin Hood sketches, so Whitmore would occasionally suggest that they go down to Brockenhurst to shoot them. The location was ideal, with expansive greenery and woodland. 'I thnk that Dave loved taking the mickey out of the Robin Hood myth', Whitmore recalled. 'In the morning we might knock off ten Robin Hood sketches, which was easy as Dave and the actors performed them without change of costume.' On another occasion, the crew clustered around under a giant chestnut tree overlooking the Thames at Bisham Abbey in Berkshire. As a single swan glided downstream, Allen, in scarlet cloak and chainmail trousers, held his helmet on his hip. Through his beard came a hint of a quizzical expression. Moments later, another Henry IV gag was in the can.

It looked impressive, but it couldn't match his high jinks at the previous location: Allen thundering into Maidenhead station like a charioteer, standing on the roof of the train with the reins in one hand and a twelve-foot wooden lance in the other. Although Peter Whitmore realized that it was freezing weather, the comedian shrugged and recalled doing fifteen takes on a sculling shot in mid-winter with ice on the ground.

By the time February came round, the series was about to be screened, and they had nearly three hundred sketches in the can. 'It wasn't a wasteful thing to do,' said Whitmore, 'for we intended using all of them through the series.' Overall, it wasn't a very costly series to produce. Allen wanted no dancers, singers or jugglers, just himself and the sketches; and the actors were relative unknowns.

After the screening of the first show in the series, Whitmore became convinced that it would soon top the ratings. 'I felt from the beginning we were on to a success', he recalls. 'For one thing, the studio audience found it very funny and this was an outstanding indicator. They laughed at Dave's story-telling and found the sketches often hilariously funny.' The critics commented on the new technique used in the series and thought it was an exciting innovation.

Whitmore attributed much of the success to the fact that when viewers tuned into *Dave Allen at Large* they never knew what to expect from the comedian. They had been careful to avoid anything crude or vulgar, and although Allen took swipes at religion and other sacred cows, he did it with a twinkle in his eye. Only once was there any trouble with a sketch. Bill Cotton had come along to see a recording and laughed a good deal at one sketch in which Allen, in bishop's robes, is intoning in deep, resonant voice a passage from the Bible as the altar boy holds the book up for him. Suddenly, the comedian's voice changes to pianissimo as the boy shuts the book – which is dangerously close to Allen's crotch – and his voice now becomes light soprano as he ends with '*Amen, amen.*'

To Whitmore, the sketch was visually very funny, but, as Cotton remarked, a bit naughty. 'You better take it out, Peter', he said, hardly able to refrain from laughing. The director, like Allen, was disappointed, but added, 'We put it back three shows later because we knew all the BBC top brass would be attending the BAFTA awards and unlikely to be looking into *Dave Allen at Large*. Funny thing is, no one ever complained or said a word about the sketch. We never, however, recorded a sketch that we thought would be offensive to viewers. I had the last word in the matter, for in those days it was rare for department heads to check on material. I knew that Dave had taste and was concerned about the quality of the comedy.'

At thirty-five, the comedian was riding the crest of the wave. Yet he refused to talk about his ambitions. As he said, 'If you have ambition and it's not realized, you'd be disappointed. But you're not if you have the understanding that you're in a business and have every intention of exploring every facet of that business.' Nor was he reluctant to talk about other comedians. 'Many have made me laugh. I think that Tony Hancock was perhaps one of the most brilliant comedians the world has ever seen. He'll be remembered for a long time. I think that people will look at Hancock like they look at Buster Keaton.'

He was reflecting on comedy with Myles Palmer of the *Radio Times*, and went on to reveal his fondness for Laurel and Hardy. 'They were perhaps the first men to use the technique of talking directly to the camera. They used it like a television camera is used now. Morecambe and Wise I find extremely funny. The lovely thing that has happened to them is that they are not a straight man and a comic. They are now two very funny men who complement one another. Admittedly there is the straighter of the two, but it's not like the Bud Abbot – Lou Costello image, where one was very strict and hard, slightly bullying.'

At that time, Allen was of the view that people were inclined to analyse comedy too much. Comedy was what made people laugh. If it was laughter you got from the person, that was comedy. If it wasn't laughter, then it was tragedy. He agreed that material was always a problem since nothing had a shorter life than a joke. 'A new gag is one you've never heard before. An old gag is one you've heard once.'

During the making of *Dave Allen at Large*, Peter Whitmore had become friendly with the comedian but he avoided any socializing. In quieter moments, he tried to analyse his gifts, or, as the public described it, the Dave Allen Phenomenon. He concluded that no one could tell a joke like the Irishman. It was a natural gift and simply couldn't be taught. It was a very rare gift and Allen knew how to exploit it. As a person, he was sincere and good company, and as a colleague, most loyal.

Despite his fame, Allen still shunned publicity and jealously guarded his private life. At his home in Hampstead, Judith was happy caring for their three children, and was not interested in pursuing her acting career. They were a happy family, even if Allen himself was sometimes described as a workaholic and a man of moods. In the summer he found time to bring the children for walks, and Judith usually accompanied him to parties.

At that time, one of the favourite butts for jokes against himself was the top of a finger missing from his left hand.

He did not hesitate to talk about the missing finger, but he refused to reveal the true story. 'If I told anyone how I lost it I would be depriving myself of a series of stories', he joked. One friend said that Allen had caught his finger in the door of his car as someone slammed it. Someone else surmised that he had accidentally chopped it off as he prepared vegetables in his Hampstead kitchen. But he usually managed to switch the conversation back to *Dave Allen at Large*, a subtle art in itself. He was happy with Peter Whitmore's direction. As he recalled, 'Peter and I play what we call Happy Families. We don't film a sketch for a particular programme. We build up a library and have a card filing system in a box. Each sketch has a code name that only Peter and I understand and when we come to plan a show we spread the cards on the table and decide on the general theme to run through a show.'

Philip Oakes in the *People* thought that Allen was by now 'the best chatman on TV', and that *Dave Allen at Large* would soon win an award. When Oakes asked the comedian why he told gags about God, the Pope and religion, he replied, 'I don't go out and pick a subject and say I'll tell a joke about that. It's just because these are subjects we talk about. It's like most things in life, you talk about them so that you can joke about them. If you can't talk about God, what is He there for?'

He admitted that he received some letters of complaint, but not a great many. They came from people who said they hadn't enjoyed a show in the series because they objected to a certain gag. Usually they didn't like his gags about the confessional box or Ireland. However, he did get complimentary letters from both parts of Ireland, so he reckoned he couldn't be offending too many people over there. For the new series he had had only a few letters of complaint – and from ten million viewers that wasn't bad.

The success of *Dave Allen at Large* was undoubtedly a source of irritation to Thames Television. They had had the chance to sign up the comedian a few years before, but never did. Allen had told them, 'I want a show where I can chat and do sketches and not be particularly involved with guests or dancing girls. They agreed to do it and called it

Inside the Mind of Dave Allen. The show was panned and I think after that they didn't want to talk about contracts.'

What he hadn't known was that Bill Cotton watched the series closely and decided that his talent could be deployed perhaps more advantageously by the BBC. Cotton says today, 'Dave looked great on the box and his black humour had a Hancock touch about it. He was, I suppose, Hancock and Benny wrapped into one. I knew he was right for a type of show like *Dave Allen at Large* where his talent could be used in zany sketches. Peter Whitmore agreed.'

After the last of the six shows had been screened by BBC2, Allen was free to accept cabaret and theatre engagements. He was careful not to overexpose himself on TV, and it was this cautious attitude that prompted both Cotton and Whitmore to say that it would help his durability as a TV comic. Cabaret appealed to him and suited his intimate style of chat. After the long months working on his TV series, it meant he could relax once again, and he welcomed the contrast it provided.

In April 1971, he was engaged to play the Talk of the Town in Leicester Square, one of the best nightclubs in the country. With its 25-foot square stage providing a full view on three sides for the audience, it was ideally suited to the comedian's style as he sat on his high stool and regaled the diners with jokes and gags. 'The venue was terrific for Dave', recalls Ernest Maxin. 'The audience was fairly close to him and he quickly created the right mood. I loved him there.'

The Talk of the Town had been the dream of the Grades and was opened in 1958 with guest stars like Anna Neagle, Vera Lynn, Max Bygraves, Shirley Bassey and Donald Wolfit. The idea behind the club was to give the man in the street a night out he would enjoy and remember. Allen had heard about it in the late 1950s as he struggled to make a name for himself in the drab North of England clubs. As he recalled, 'Like every other comic in England, my ambition was one day to play the Talk of the Town. I regarded it as the posh club, the one place where you were seen by the top impresarios of the day.'

First-night audiences could be intolerant of stars who they reckoned hadn't given full value for money. But this was the exception. Sophie Tucker, although in her seventies, held the audience spellbound. When she came on first they didn't know what to expect, but once she sang 'Life Begins at Forty' they adored her. It was the same with Frankie Vaughan who created a magical atmosphere. Lew Grade made no secret of his admiration for Allen's comedy gifts and wanted him for the Talk of the Town. As he said, 'Dave's got star quality and that's what the diners want at the Town.'

On his high stool he looked relaxed as he became a social satirist for some minutes, then switched happily to bishop of his flock. The audience sat enthralled. He never tried to antagonize them nor insult them when they failed to laugh. He found such an approach wrong. He came on after the 800 people present had dined and chatted their way through the main course. They were now in the mood to listen and because the comedian's best jokes were long with funny punchlines it meant they could digest the food without an instant riot of laughter.

To Allen, it was the perfect cabaret setting and he enjoyed it. Smooth and sophisticated, he spoke with a soft Irish lilt about God, sex, the Devil and hell. As he said, 'For cabaret, I can take my time. Work a subject up. I don't practise my gags on my wife or my friends. I practise them on the audience. If the audience likes the jokes, they stay.'

Among the critics who went along to the Town on that April evening was John Barber of the *Daily Telegraph*, one of the first Fleet Street journalists to discover the genius of comedian Ken Dodd. He reminded his readers that Allen was Irish and had much to say about the local superstitiousness, drunkenness, and rainfall ('If you see an Irishman with a tan, it's rust'). And about priests and celibacy, the comic was wincingly rude and rather funny. About the Pope, he was defensive and – to Barber, who wasn't a Catholic – not funny at all.

The critic continued:

Mr Allen then selects an Irish Protestant, a Catholic and a Jew from his audience, and rewards each with a glass of champagne for allowing them to be his butts. The Scots get off lightly – they are merely denounced as hairy heathens.

Some of his long rustic anecdotes have the charm of a good rough wine, and Mr. Allen is particularly satisfying at the ancient art of impersonating drunks returning home to abominable wives. But all his jibes and jeers are spun out for a long hour, the comedian never abandoning the stage or his microphone, and never doing anything but talk. It is a pleasure to find an entertainer with some sort of political convictions, even if his anti-immigrant jokes are dubious and his taste non-existent.

From the tone of his review, published under the heading, 'DAVE ALLEN'S CHARM INCLUDES INSULTS', it was clear that Barber left the Talk of the Town with some personal reservations about Dave Allen, the cabaret artist. He would further state in his review that, 'the comedian ingratiates himself with the audience by insulting them in all directions. He puts himself across as one of those blisteringly honest fellows who look you straight in the eye while defaming your race, nationality and religion – and then holds out a sporty hand for you to shake.'

The critic was taking a distinctly opposite view to Allen himself, who always went out of his way to assert that he never deliberately insulted audiences. There was no reason, he said, why he should adopt that destructive course.

To Allen, his act was merely a series of funny insights into subjects people talked about, and he tried to ensure that his humour was both subtle and original. If people interpreted these 'insights' as insults then that was their affair. The Grades, whose Talk of the Talk had become a comedy landmark, had complete faith in the comedian's cabaret act.

Allen considered himself a versatile performer and success at the top rung of the cabaret scene was as important to him as his television fame. Soon he would be hoping to extend his talents further.

12   Royal Court Début

If, by 1972, his film career was going nowhere, it did not mean he was in a rut. That autumn, when he was offered a part in a new play, he accepted it. 'I read it and I decided to do it,' Allen recalls. 'It is good to change attack, by changing attack and exploring it has to be beneficial to whatever you are doing. I don't intend to change gear totally, but I want to experiment and, in experimenting, get better at what I'm doing.'

There is nothing new in a comedian deciding to go 'straight'. George Robey's Falstaff won critical acclaim, Frankie Howerd was admired as Bottom in *A Midsummer Night's Dream*, and Ken Dodd surprised Merseysiders by playing Malvolio in *Twelfth Night*. There's an old saying in show-business that inside every great clown there lurks a great dramatic actor anxious to get out. In some people's minds it does not seem enough, though, for a comedian to excel in the exacting, disciplined and difficult art of making people laugh – he must also secretly yearn to make people cry.

It would be Allen's first straight role. He was asked to portray Dr Daly in Edna O'Brien's new play, *A Pagan Place*. The doctor is a sombre but wise medical man. Director Ronald Eyre had sent the comedian the script. 'Dave was my first choice', he says today. 'It always seemed to me a good idea to have something a bit arresting in a cast and he filled that role.'

Eyre had first met Allen when he directed *Veterans* at the Royal Court Theatre with John Gielgud in the cast. Afterwards, Allen and his wife Judith – a friend of Gielgud's – joined Eyre for a drink and a chat about the

Charles Wood play. Eyre was always aware that the comedian wanted to be considered for some straight acting; he was never someone who looked on from outside.

To the director, Allen was, theatrically, an insider – very involved, serious, wrapped up in it. He remembers that he accepted a part in *A Pagan Place* very fast, in fact he was one of the first to be cast. The real problem was finding a young girl to portray Creena, the twelve-year-old girl, for the action is seen primarily through her eyes. By now the search had extended to Ireland. In Dublin, where Edna O'Brien was holidaying, she explained that they were looking for an Irish girl aged twelve who had the qualities of wisdom and simplicity. Eventually they found the girl to play the part in Dublin.

Veronica Quilligan was still at school when her teacher decided to put her forward for audition. She was sixteen and very keen to follow a career in drama or ballet. During the audition in London with Ronald Eyre, she was asked to recite a poem and speak some lines from a play. Miss O'Brien was present and thought the girl looked younger than her age. This was one of the factors that helped her get the much coveted role.

It was a busy time for Miss O'Brien. She had been disappointed that her play had been turned down by the Dublin Theatre Festival, but was pleased that Ronald Eyre was directing it for the Royal Court, and that Allen had agreed to play the doctor. 'I expect that he will be very good in the part', she told Eyre. That autumn, her novel *Night* was published, and she admitted that she suffered from 'an excess of energy.'

At that time, she lived in a big house in a green Chelsea square, with her two sons, Sacha and Carlos. London appealed to her. 'I can work in London because here I feel myself a stranger and keep myself a stranger.' Recognized as a leading novelist, she was now anxious to make her way in the theatre, though she agreed that it would be a difficult path. She attended the rehearsals at the Irish Club in Eaton Square, a stone's throw from the Royal Court Theatre in Sloane Square. They were held in a spacious room on the first floor and it was soon evident that Allen was determined to be seen merely as one of the cast, not as an international comic. Since few, if any of the cast knew him, they in turn wondered how he would react to them. They admired his work on television and he was regarded as 'a very funny man.'

When Veronica Quilligan was introduced to the star on the first day of rehearsals she looked at him in awe. 'I was awestruck by his reputation,' she recalls, 'but he did not act the big star at all. As the days went by, he was encouraging to me.' Patrick Dawson, who had a small part in the play, found the comedian polite and genial, and not funny at all. What struck him was the hard work Allen was prepared to put into rehearsals. Some days, Edna O'Brien and designer Sean Kenny attended as attentive observers.

Sometimes at a break the cast went downstairs to the bar and had coffee and sandwiches. It was here that they got to know Allen better, though the comedian spoke quietly and never tried to be funny. To Ronald Eyre, he was no problem at all:

Dave worked very quietly. He never lost concentration at rehearsals. Didn't just want to be buttered up, and valued straight talking when it was called for. I never for a moment felt any doubt that he would be good. I knew that those who expected him to do something comic and anarchic would be disappointed on the night. In fact, I remember telling him that he didn't have to throw overboard all the solo techniques he'd got famous on – they could feed the acting. I don't think he was very convinced and plotted out his performance without cutting corners resorting to proven routines.

Miss Quilligan, who appreciated the advice she got from Miss O'Brien about her role in the play, was on her own admission in awe of the novelist because she was so beautiful. 'She was like a fairy godmother to me', she says. 'I was delighted and thrilled by her. If I asked her a question she would always try to answer it logically and without fuss.' The rehearsals proceeded smoothly, Patrick Dawson remembers, 'I don't think there was any real problem.' Once, Miss Quilligan upset Eyre while he rehearsed a scene in which she had to pretend she was Clark Gable. As the director showed her how to play the scene, she finally began to mimic his performance, and he came down on her 'like a ton of bricks'.

Eyre invited the actor Alec Guinness to attend the final rehearsal. 'He listened very attentively to what we were saying,' remembers Dawson, 'and when we had finished, he spoke to us collectively.' Guinness, a devout Catholic, was interested in the sentiments the play's theme expressed. He did not try to pick out Allen for individual attention, except exchange a brief word or two with him.

There was a decidedly Irish flavour about the first night. Allen's début as a straight actor had aroused a good deal of curiosity, and some notable Irish actors in London attended. Miss Quilligan's parents travelled from Dublin, and Allen's own wife and family were present. Next morning the young heroine stole the reviews, and one evening paper headlined her performance, 'A STAR IS BORN AT THE ROYAL COURT'.

'I thought she was wonderfully self-confident', says Patrick Dawson. 'I think that all of us in the rest of the cast were also delighted by Dave Allen's assured performance. He was unrecognizable from the comedian on TV. I'm sure anyone watching *A Pagan Place* would never believe he was an international comic. He really got inside the role.'

For a girl of sixteen it was an overwhelming experience. Miss Quilligan remembers everybody trying to shake her hand at once, and her parents fussing over her. 'I was fortunate to have Ronald Eyre directing me in my first stage role', she says. 'He was thorough and imaginative. Playing opposite Dave Allen was for me an extraordinary experience. He never tried to upstage me. As the doctor he was very natural. The play afforded me great scope to express myself.' Since the cast was listed in the programme in alphabetical order, it meant that Allen's name came first, and the comedian had a quiet laugh at that. Harold Hobson, one of the most influential critics of the day, reviewed the play for the *Sunday Times* and succinctly summed up, 'If there is a better play than this in London, then London must be extremely lucky.' His brief review read:

> A wake in an Irish public house, a picnic by the sea, the revival of an old passion, when a doctor calls on a middle-aged patient, a lesson by an eccentric schoolmaster, the conversations of a profligate priest with a young girl – Miss O'Brien makes of these apparently disconnected things a vision of life that is delicate and touching, illuminated by the light of a memory that is calmed but not assuaged.

Hobson praised Ronald Eyre's direction and the acting by the cast, and continued, 'Dave Allen is notable for his resigned *gravitas*, and Veronica Quilligan for her serene childlike wisdom'.

Robert Berestein in *The Observer* was more concerned about the general theatrical scene. 'Dare I say it …The English theatre seems to be in a little trouble. London has been considered the theatrical centre of the world for so long that perhaps it has escaped notice that the centre isn't holding very well any more.'

There were some mixed reviews from the Irish critics present at the Royal Court. David Brazil, representing the *Irish Press* thought that Allen was a revelation as the sombre doctor. 'An excellent portrayal', he described his performance. 'Allen portrays him as a wise medical man, on whose shoulders weigh heavily the burden of disappointment with life, expressed in cynicism towards the people he treats as patients.'

Brazil was also deeply impressed by Miss Quilligan's performance. As he wrote, 'She effectively portrays juvenile bemusement with her elders. Her self-confidence and style on the stage stop just short of precocity, and how she is going to be content with school again I do not know.'

Few could have been prepared for the damning *Irish*

Times review. The paper sent along its London-based representative James Downey whose views bore scant resemblance to his fellow critics. Downey stated:

> There can be few parallels for the artistic atrocity now being perpetrated by Miss Edna O'Brien, Mr Ronald Eyre and others at the Royal Court, Sloane Square, London. The theme of *A Pagan Place* is the familiar theme of Miss O'Brien's childhood, the locale, the equally familiar locale of Miss O'Brien's native Clare soil. The characters are again familiar, the principals being Miss O'Brien (at the age of twelve) plus her father, her sister, the doctor and so on. A nauseous rehash is presented of the usual topics: the child's mechanistic innocence, the father's decayed gentility, the sister's predictable tragedy, the doctor's seediness, the priest's lust, set in the context of rural brutality, squalor and ignorance. It is all the more repulsive for the tiny illuminations of insight and artistic sensitivity that from time to time break through its monstrous boredom and vulgarity. It does not appear to be possible for Miss O'Brien to be absolutely a bad writer, though she has certainly tried very hard on this occasion. She has an intense feeling of period – in this case 1945. She has a genuine ability to encapsulate a bit of life, at a certain time and place, and she understands a great deal about childhood. But all this serves only to point up the thinness of her characterization, the absurdity of the plot and the general pointlessness of the entire evening.

Downey thought that the performance by the cast was worthy of a better vehicle, and in picking out Miss Quilligan for mention did concede, 'It must be said in all fairness that the very remarkable playing by Veronica Quilligan in the part of the child could hardly have been possible without the real talent of Miss O'Brien herself, a talent which she grossly betrayed in this farrago.'

Downey's review was read avidly in Ireland, and the Dublin Theatre Festival's decision to reject the play now seemed fully justified. But he did not answer the question on everyone's lips, 'What of Dave Allen's début as a straight actor?' He was not the only critic to ignore the international star comedian. Miss O'Brien was not provoked by the review, but a few days later an angry reader in Middlesex wrote to the editor of the *Irish Times*:

> Miss O'Brien and Ronald Eyre have together achieved a memorable stage experience, evoking a rural childhood in a series of almost photographic scenes so that one tends to view the pictures in sepia and what can be more beautiful than that?

Despite the mixed reviews, *A Pagan Place* had a successful run at the Royal Court, and in theatrical eyes, Allen, like Robey, Howerd and Dodd before him, had made the difficult transition from comic to straight actor successfully. Miss Quilligan was among the first to congratulate him on his performance. 'I thought he was marvellous', she says today, nearly nineteen years after her own début. Ronald Eyre is convinced that Allen could have made a living as a straight actor. 'Whether it would have given him the sort of fame he's had, I couldn't say', he reflected. 'There is a great privateness about him on stage – whether solo or in a play – and that's alluring to watch. You're always wanting to sort of get behind him and see what the other side's like. There's an air of danger about him. That's very arresting. To work with, I'd say his trump card is that, like an iceberg, you're never sure what sort of continent is lying concealed. You're never in any doubt that the sub-continent is there, but you never quite know its features.'

Ernest Maxin was of the same opinion as Eyre and felt that Allen could make a living as a straight actor. He saw him as an actor-comedian, capable of playing comedy or thriller roles on stage or in movies. He was in no way surprised by his success at the Royal Court. 'I expected it all the time', he says. 'Dave Allen is simply a very fine actor, apart from comedy altogether.' Equally, Peter Whitmore, who had worked with him in *Dave Allen at Large* was not surprised, and thought that perhaps he should do more plays. 'Versatility is one of Dave's great assets', he mused.

In retrospect, James Downey, who now works as a

journalist in Dublin, still feels that *A Pagan Place* was pretty bad and stands over what he wrote about it:

> It's a long time since I saw the play, but I believe that Veronica Quilligan's talents were wasted in it. I did not expect however the strong reaction to my review from Miss O'Brien's friends. At a party in journalist Mary Kenny's house in London a few days after the play's première I was confronted by actor T.P.McKenna who took exception to what I had written in the *Irish Times*, and accused me of misjudging the worth of the play. I remember I argued my point strongly and asserted that in my view it was not really a play at all, rather more a series of dramatic episodes strung together. A few more of Miss O'Brien's friends thought I had done Edna O'Brien a serious misjustice. I told them that I felt entitled to write honestly about what I saw on stage.

In her London flat in 1989, Veronica Quilligan still had the autographed copy of *A Pagan Place* given to her by Miss O'Brien during rehearsals. 'I have read all of her books', says Miss Quilligan. She has remained a friend of the Irish novelist, and regrets that she hasn't written more for the theatre.

Some of her friends in Ireland were surprised that Edna O'Brien had not tackled James Downey about his review of her play, but throughout the controversy she observed what friends said was 'a dignified silence'.

Allen expressed satisfaction with his own performance in the play, but he tended, on his own admission, to 'go with the current' and refused to plan ahead with straight parts in mind. At times, he became restless, and thought of Australia or a nationwide tour of his solo show. 'I don't like preplanning', he said more than once. It was true. When the next challenge came along, he was inclined to say yes. Anyway it was extremely doubtful, as in Ken Dodd's case, that the theatre with its great insecurity could provide the kind of money he had become accustomed to. If he was disappointed with the way his movie ambitions had evaporated, he was not disappointed with life. He still had enough zest for living to want to tackle new projects, though it was significant that after his début as an actor at the Royal Court, he told a reporter, 'I'm not switching. I'm not totally swapping from one to the other.'

13   A Nun's Story

For Peter Whitmore, these were happy times. Working on *Dave Allen at Large* gave him the stimulus he needed, and by March 1973 he was saying, 'None of us knew how successful the series was going to be. I think it surpassed all our expectations.'

Even today, eighteen years later, Whitmore talks enthusiastically about the ratings for the series. At that time, it was pulling in ten million viewers for each show, which was a record for a light entertainment series on BBC2. Amazingly, considering that number, there were few outraged missives, no jammed switchboards, no threats of excommunication, only viewers determined to be in front of the box for the next screening.

To Whitmore, Allen was an incredible story-teller with an endless supply of jokes and gags. The show's format remained the same. Each show had about thirty taped items, and a series of six shows drew upon a 'bank' of about 250 taped sketches, with virtually any selection being suitable for any show, as no great attempt was made to give each programme a special theme. Although *Dave Allen at Large* was not a costly show to produce, Whitmore confirmed that, 'the comedian did not come cheap'.

Together, they worked smoothly as a team. Allen was never reluctant to talk about the series. 'I enjoy the chat and the gags to the live audience best of all, although the filming can be good fun, especially as we have a regular team which has been together from our previous series.'

Whitmore continued to be surprised by the sheer hard work that the comedian put into the series, his utter dedication. While he worked on the show he took no outside engagements, refusing invitations to guest on other TV chat-shows. Whitmore considered it a sensible outlook. As he said, 'I knew that Dave went out of his way to avoid overexposure. He was very wise.' The producer was elated by the good reaction of viewers and the joy the series was obviously giving them. Like the studio audience, he had to admit that he sometimes laughed at the comedian's jokes. One, in particular, amused him no end. It concerned Sister Bernadette who is telling a reporter about her experience in an Italian convent during the war.

Sister B.: I tell you it was terrible. First the Italian Army advanced, swept through our convent and raped me and the rest of the nuns. All except Sister Mathilda. Then the German Army swept through the area, came to the convent and again we were all raped. All except Sister Mathilda.

Reporter: My God, it must have been horrifying!

Sister B.: Yes, but then the two armies were later forced to retreat. Again they came through our convent, and twice more we were raped. All except Sister Mathilda.

Reporter: (moved to tears) How dreadful! But how was it that Sister Mathilda escaped being raped?

Sister B.: Well, you see, Sister Mathilda doesn't much like that sort of thing.

Evidently, such a joke could be expected to cause offence to some people, never mind nuns in a convent, yet curiously there were only two or three letters of complaint, and none of them from nuns. To Whitmore, it was the funny punchline that 'saved the day', and it was another example of Allen's technique and original style. Undeniably, a sense of style was important to the comedian and he himself thought it evolved itself. 'It's not something you think about,' he explained, 'or at least it's not something I have thought about. Once you start analysing your technique or even the gags themselves, then I think you just go round and round in circles.'

When it came to humour, there was no holy ground he

was not prepared to touch. God, the Church, sex, drink –
they all continued to get the Allen treatment. Some critics
were surprised that he got away with it. 'There's enough
blasphemy to keep the Spanish Inquisition in kindling for
months', commented one critic.

Allen was pleased that he was attracting the biggest
audience on BBC2, but hardly overwhelmed. As he
reflected, 'The only thing these figures do is set you a
target. You hope you can retain it. But basically what I'm
there for is enjoyment – mine and theirs. The pleasure the
show gives is more important to me than the numbers
who watch it.'

He still wrote seventy per cent of his own material, with
Austin Steele and Peter Vincent scripting the rest. To
director Peter Whitmore, Allen was full of ideas and they
never had any trouble filling the sketch slots, 'Dave went
out of his way to find the unusual – and it worked.' But he
had to agree that the comedian lived dangerously, and
that any day soon they expected a complaint from the
Vatican.

Off the set, they lunched together and, as always,
Whitmore found the comedian genial company. There,
their socializing ended, and for the most part they went
their separate ways at night. 'I wanted it no other way',
recalls the director. 'In this way, I found our relationship
retained its freshness.'

If these were happy times for Whitmore, the same was
true for the comedian. Judith still stayed at home to mind
the children and remained very supportive of her
husband. As long as he needed her to care for the
children, and look after their home in Hampstead, she
would sacrifice her TV and stage careers. It wasn't an easy
choice for her. At the time of her marriage her career was
nearing a peak, but like her husband she wanted children
and was prepared to exchange fame and glamour for the
more humdrum role of housewife.

A realist, Judith recognized that comedians were a breed
apart in show-business. Off-stage, they were often not the
funniest of people, and some of them could be impractical,
like her own husband. By now she accepted him as a star

entertainer whose life entailed hard work and travel, and she did not object when he went to Australia or undertook tours in Britain. Marriage to a comedian would never be easy. Laughter and frustration were integral facets of their careers, depending on how their careers were faring. In the summer, though, her husband found time to bring the family to the country for walks and he was good with children. Judith realized that it was important for him to distance himself occasionally from the studio and cabaret scene. In his own way he was able to relax, yet his moods could vary from bright to dark. But she had learned to cope.

Sport meant a good deal to the comedian. All his life, he has retained an abiding interest in cricket and rugby, and he could say that sport afforded him much pleasure. Occasionally he liked to use it as a butt for jokes, as he did with rugby which he loved from boyhood. He derived malicious delight from telling the tale about the three fellows watching a game in Dublin. Ireland were pressing the English line. The crowd were shouting and swaying. One of the trio suddenly keeled over and died in the excitement. Pat turns to his mate and says, 'Shaun has died.' Comes the reply, 'God, he's missing the best part of the match.'

He confesses that the discovery of girls put an abrupt end to his own sports career.

By late summer of that year, 1973, he was preparing to fly to Sydney for a number of engagements. It was not the most suitable time as he was leaving Judith and the children behind. He was relieved, however, by the news that the Australian Broadcasting Control Board had lifted its two-year ban on his live performances, so leaving him free to go ahead with two live *Tonight* shows for Channel Nine.

Two years before, the ban had been imposed on him after he hosted a special TV show with Peter Cook and Dudley Moore as his star guests. There were strong complaints from viewers about the remarks made by the trio on the nationally broadcast show. They complained about references to masturbation, homosexuality and swearing. Both Cook and Moore denied making anti-Semitic remarks on the show.

When Allen arrived at Sydney airport on that September afternoon, he said he hoped that whole 'incident' would be soon forgotten as he wanted to get on with his *Tonight* show. Nonetheless, this *cause célèbre* of broadcasting would not go away so easily and again he was quizzed. Public interest was understandable. It had been the first time in twenty years that such a ban had been imposed on performers. The Broadcasting Control Board had sent telegrams to all TV stations throughout Australia advising them that in future any items by Allen, Cook and Moore must be prerecorded and censored by a responsible executive before being aired.

It was a blow to Allen's prestige as a TV host and spotlighted a certain irresponsibility in his make-up, a lack of reliability, perhaps, in the eyes of more conservative viewers. His performance, as well as that of Cook and Moore, raised questions in television itself about the wisdom of giving star performers too much rope. In lifting the ban on Allen the board had not entirely forgiven him. It had agreed to the live shows only on condition that a responsible Channel Nine executive remain in the control room throughout the programme. Presumably the executive was to stop transmission of the programme if Allen didn't toe the line. It was impossible to edit material from live performances.

Allen, who was anxious to maintain his lucrative working links with Australian television, saw no problem arising and did not feel restricted by the 'sit in' executive. Earlier, at the airport, he talked about the show and was surprised to be asked if he was going to make his singing début. He laughed as he said that his voice was produced from the throat and had no resonance. He was a talker, an interviewer, a comedian, but not a singer. 'I don't even sing in my bath', he assured the eager press corps.

Since the imposition of the broadcast ban, his popularity had by no means waned, though it was true that some people now wondered if he could be entirely trusted as a TV host. His star reputation in Britain had preceded him, and columnists speculated about his visit to Australia and whether he wanted to spend more time among them. The comedian denied this was true. Most of them saw him as, 'a loveable clown' and 'a great joker', and they reckoned that he was indebted to Australia for making him a star. Allen would not be drawn about his private life, except to say he had two children and that he and Judith were happily married. He risked boring newspaper readers by talking about his early days in Ireland and explaining how he achieved his breakthrough in Britain; what most of them wanted were revelations about himself and his love for Judith.

Australians by now saw him essentially as a talker, at once imperturbable and charming, a man who was hard to dislike.

The thing that endeared him to Australians was his refusal to change, despite his rising fame. The absence of ego never failed to puzzle them. Allen remained a down-to-earth entertainer who almost seemed reluctant to enjoy the trappings of stardom and flout its symbols. His *Tonight* shows went out without a hitch and there was never any danger that the 'sit in' executive would pull the plug on him.

It was a fruitful time for Allen. As he flew out of Sydney airport, he was already thinking of his West End date with actress Maggie Smith. They were cast as the stars of *Peter Pan*, and that was something that excited him. As an actress, she was one of his favourites, a woman of outstanding talent. He loved challenges, and he saw his role of Captain Hook as yet another test of his own versatility. He could not wait to begin rehearsals.

14   Captain Hook

In November 1973, Allen was at the peak of his popularity. Some suggested he was capitalizing on his success in *Dave Allen at Large*, and it was partly true; more to the point however was the prospect of co-starring with Maggie Smith in *Peter Pan*. To Allen, it had a dream ring about it. It promised to be a lively Christmas entertainment scene. Spike Milligan would star in *Treasure Island* at the Mermaid Theatre, Danny La Rue topped the bill at the Prince of Wales, and comedian Frankie Howerd was in the cast of *Jack and the Beanstalk* at the Palladium.

Unsurprisingly, playgoers were curious at Maggie Smith's decision to play the title role in *Peter Pan*. Up to then she had made her reputation in classic roles, playing Desdemona to Laurence Olivier's Othello at the Old Vic, for example; but in the 1950s she had been hailed as a brilliant comedienne; in both comedy and classic drama she had won many awards. She looked fragile and ethereal, yet at rehearsals for a play she became incisive, rigorous, inexhaustible. She refused to reveal, discuss or analyse the way she worked. 'If you stop to think how you do it you couldn't do it', she protested.

A year before, in 1972, Maggie Smith appeared with her husband, Robert Stephens, in Noël Coward's *Private Lives*, and though it was a commercial success, it did not prove a particularly happy experience. At that time, her marriage began to break down and in distress she left England for Stratford, Ontario, to join the theatre company there.

Now Maggie Smith was back again, and in more relaxed mood. She had happily accepted the invitation to be Peter Pan because of the pleasure her own children had taken in the play the previous Christmas. She was also an old friend of Allen and his wife Judith Stott, and she said she looked forward to playing for the first time opposite him. They had more in common than met the eye. Like the comedian, she didn't play the star, and off-stage led a quiet, private life, refusing to talk about her marriage to the popular press. As an actress, she was also a perfectionist, given, like Allen, to exploring every detail of the part she was to play on stage or on screen.

To prepare for the high-flying Peter Pan, she went to Wolverhampton to test her flying equipment. A Spanish expert named Miguel, a former trapeze artist, was waiting on the stage of the Wolverhampton theatre with her flying harness. He proceeded to climb up a couple of steps and then leapt out to a rope. When he caught the rope, she went up. For hours she worked at it until she got the hang of it. Similarly, Allen prepared for the role of Captain Hook with typical dedication. He got special lessons to improve his skills at sword play, and assured Miss Smith that by the first night he would be the equal of Errol Flynn.

Rehearsing the sword scenes was both tough and amusing. After a week of rehearsal, they were still not models of perfection. 'We cling to each other', said the red-haired actress. 'How can you cross swords with a hook. There's all this terrible counting and ducking and jumping and then running ... ' The giant Coliseum theatre had its hazards. To Allen, it was enormous, almost impersonal, and he wondered whether *Peter Pan* would get lost in it. Miss Smith thought the stage itself very big and it rather terrified her. 'The orchestra pit looked five miles away', she recalls. 'I had to lower my voice to a high-pitched scream.'

Despite the theatre's size, the run of the show was almost sold out when booking opened early in December. Those who remembered Miss Smith in plays such as *Mary Mary*, *Hedda Gabler* and *The Way of the World* would naturally want to see her performance as the legendary Peter Pan, while film-goers had not forgotten her great success in *The Prime of Miss Jean Brodie*. Allen fans identified him more as a TV comic, yet they reasoned that

the role of Captain Hook was up his street, blending as it
did agility with stage assurance.

While the critics praised the cast, they had some harsh
things to say about the production; although Ian Christie
in the *Daily Express* remarked,

> The production by Robert Helpmann is staged engagingly
> by Alan Pinniger and in spite of inadequate amplification
> in the early part of the show and the presence of a
> vociferous lunatic in the gods the opening was a huge
> success. In visual terms the enterprise constantly delights
> and astonishes the eyeballs – the flying scenes being
> particularly effortless and poetic.

Christie singled out the performances by Allen and Miss
Smith. 'Dave Allen is an admirable choice for the leading
man,' he said. 'He bumbles amiably about the stage as Mr
Darling and plays the villainous Captain Hook to such
effect that the audience hissed like a collection of
punctured tyres.' Likewise, Christie was captivated by
Maggie Smith. 'She plays the boy who has no intention of
ever growing up and she flies through the part with the
greatest of ease. She has just the right blend of boyishness
and buoyancy, arrogance and vulnerability that the part
requires.'

Irving Wardle in *The Times* was far from pleased with the
production, which he described as 'another lame,
undercast, wretchedly stage-managed version of a play
which in any case could never get across properly in a
theatre the size of the Coliseum.' It had, in his view,
opened inaudibly, and his further enjoyment was not
helped by an enraged female voice in the circle. 'Don't you
tell me to shush', it said, 'with your son hitting me across
the face because you showed him how to do it', and much
more in the same vein, provoking shouts of 'Out, out!'
from other customers.

Wardle thought that Miss Smith cut a buccaneer-like
figure as Peter Pan and lit up the adventures with flashes
of mischief. Of Captain Hook, he wrote: 'Dave Allen
substitutes a reedy thin-blooded master-mind for the

A pensive Allen surveys his audience

Opposite: Rehearsing for
first pantomime with act.
Maggie Smith in the West

Edna O'Brien was happy with
the casting of the comedian in
her play *A Pagan Place*

Ronald Eyre directed the
comedian in his first 'straight'
stage role

Bishop Empey invited the comedian on his TV show in Ireland,
a decision that surprised some Irish viewers

Allen relaxes in the garden
of his home in Kensington

Allen in full regalia as the
high-ranking prelate, a role
that the clergy did not
always like

Champagne for the star at the Theatre Royal, Norwich, with
Dick Condon (manager) and G. Mitchel of the Victoria

Home is the hero for Allen who
guards his privacy with
utmost zeal

Allen displays the mastery of his solo act with simple but expressive gestures

usual rambling villain. Often he seems to be walking on invisible chalk. But it is neither his fault nor Miss Smith's that climaxes, like the fight on the pirate ship, are staged so messily as to obliterate the plot'.

As in the case of the Edna O'Brien play, *A Pagan Place*, Allen emerged from *Peter Pan* with his reputation as a versatile artist enhanced, and he was to count his performance as among the most enjoyable of his career. When someone suggested that he take himself to Stratford-on-Avon for a season of Shakespearean drama, he didn't think the idea as absurd as it seemed. 'If they pay me well enough, I'll consider it', he said slyly. It wasn't altogether a question of money: finding the time was the real problem.

The year 1974 promised to be an extremely busy one for the comedian. BBC planned a retrospective best of his shows culled from his BBC2 series, and he agreed to do a short series with ITV called *Dave Allen in Search of Great British Eccentrics*. He hoped to complete a book, *A Little Night Reading* about his favourite horror-stories with, as he said, works by Poe, Conan Doyle, M.R.James, O'Henry and others. Bram Stoker's *The Squaw* was included, and so was Wilde's delightful *Canterville Ghost*. He attributed his interest in horror-tales to his Irish childhood and a fervent imagination, and being a good kind of Irish daylight atheist. Research for the book brought him to the Adelphi Hotel in Liverpool, and a night he described as 'jumbled and macabre' when he swore he slept with the light on. And he had the last laugh, when it became a bestseller in Christmas of that year, 1974.

Curiously, he liked to describe himself at this time as an increasingly introverted man, not the life and soul of a party, and some friends found the description accurate. When he agreed to interviews, he rarely, if ever, invited a magazine or newspaper columnist to his home. Once, he used his publisher's flat in central London, and went to pains to explain that he drew a line between his private and public lives. As always, he jealously guarded his privacy. After the surprising success of his book of horror stories, someone asked him if he ever thought of writing his memoirs. The comedian pulled a horrified face, as if he had been asked to execute his best friend, and said, 'Gosh, no'.

Much of his comedy still came from observations and exaggeration of human behaviour, such as people in traffic jams picking their noses, people talking in restaurants, politicians on the telly. He admitted that he didn't like politicians, TV commercials, traffic jams, American slang, which debased the language, or people who preferred dogs to children. He said that the religious sketches on his shows were among the most popular because of their irreverence. He seemed to keep a permanent supply: some straight jokes, some curious asides. Asked once if he wasn't afraid he'd be struck by lightning one day, he quipped, 'If God has any sense of humour, I'm the only one who's going to be in heaven. I had a thought the other day – God must be insane to make an invisible place and then put a wall and a gate around it!'

He thought more about heaven than he did about hell, though he liked to tell friends about the rabbi, the priest and the vicar descending through three stages of hell. 'At the first stage the Catholic gets out and it's all flames and arid desert. Then they go down to the Israeli hell and it's beautiful – trees, oranges, kibbutzes, everything. They go down one more level and it's like the first one, and the Anglican says to Satan, "Why do we get *these*?" "Well," says Satan, "it's those Jewish people and their irrigation." '

When in full spate, he was great company. Sometimes he liked to make outrageous statements, even his friends were taken aback. He revealed that occasionally he woke up his children during the night to tell them terrifying stories. When one listener expressed horror, the comedian pulled a funny face and said, 'It's true – and the kids love it.' Despite his idiosyncrasies, he could be a warm man. Children took him straight into their hearts. Once, walking down Crown Street in Sydney after lunch, he came across a group of terrace-house children playing hopscotch. Straight away they accepted them into the game, and taught him the rules.

At home he was close to his own children. They looked forward to his return from trips abroad so that they could invite him to a midnight feast. 'It was a secret between us,' recalled the comedian. 'Judith stayed out of it. I had a special invitation written to me, to come and open the feast. The children got the fruit, lemonade, biscuits.' At midnight he would wake them up and join them sitting on the floor as they began to eat; afterwards, he would put out the lights and they would all huddle in one or two beds. He picked a subject – a ghost-story. 'You never saw such tired children in the morning, because we were all too terrified to go to sleep', he mused.

He was proud of children, especially his own children. 'All children have good minds and vivid imaginations,' he would say, 'and I like to explore the world through their eyes.'

In the 1970s, when he was invited out to lunch by columnists, they were surprised by his choice of food. Some expected him to order exotic dishes and drink everything in sight. They were disappointed when he chose oysters and drank a glass of water. 'I'm not a daytime drinker', he reminded them. 'All I need is a glass of wine, and I could easily go to sleep. I eat and drink and chat at night.' But it was alcohol in the glass he sipped during his shows, perched on a stool. He said he wouldn't pretend to be drinking it if he wasn't.

He had completed the two programmes of the short series *Dave Allen in Search of Great British Eccentrics* and had derived a lot of fun making it. He tracked down at least one vicar who dressed up as a cowboy, and a couple whose enormous model railway was harnessed to running – entirely and indefinitely – the 1938 timetable out of St Pancras. He could scarcely believe Britain contained so many eccentrics, yet it was true, and he felt the programmes would rouse a lot of conservatives out of their lethargy. If viewers at that time realized that the comedian was a follower of the philosopher Kahlil Gibran ('The Prophet') and read him for his joy of life, they would probably class him, too, as one of Britain's Great Eccentrics. As he explained, 'It's like the philosophy of

Christ, of Buddha, or Muhammed, or any of the great philosophers.' In a self-mocking vein, he would add, 'It's basically, treat others as you would treat yourself – which is great unless you're a masochist.'

Early in 1975 the comedian found himself in trouble with the Church authorities. It arose out of a sketch on *Dave Allen at Large* when, dressed as the Pope, he did a striptease on the steps of the Vatican. At Northwich, Cheshire, five hundred parishioners at St Wilfrid's Roman Catholic Church signed a petition criticizing the show for constantly attacking the Church in both its doctrine and personnel.

Father John O'Sullivan of St Wilfrid's said that after a number of complaints from both Catholics and non-Catholics over a period about the contents of the TV series he decided to watch the show and was appalled to discover Dave Allen taking off his papal vestments to the tune of 'The Stripper'. Afterwards he telephoned the BBC's controller of programmes to voice his protest, and pointed out that in his view the show was in bad taste. Later, nearly 200,000 Catholics in the north-west were asked to join a viewers' protest to the BBC and boycott future shows by the Dublin-born comedian.

Director of the series, Peter Whitmore, was surprised by the swift reaction of the parishioners of St Wilfrid's and agreed the protest was the most concerted yet against Allen's gags and sketches. In retrospect, he says that he found the Vatican sketch very funny and certainly not in bad taste. 'As I have said before, Dave does these things with a twinkle in his eye and they are not meant to be taken seriously. *Dave Allen at Large* is essentially a comedy show.'

Allen remained unrepentant. At his Surrey home, he stated, 'If the priest and his flock were upset by the sketch I am very sorry, but there is no way I can justify the sketch to people if they found it offensive.' It was clear that in the eyes of many Catholics the comedian had gone too far on this occasion, and this was reflected in the campaign launched by Tom Elwood, a Northwich primary school headmaster to get Catholics in the Shrewsbury diocese to complain to the BBC.

The newspapers latched on to the story, and a few of them contacted some high-ranking churchmen in London who were reported as saying that they laughed along with millions of other viewers at Allen's series and did not take exception to the Vatican skit. Father Agnellus Andrew, general secretary of the Church's Mass Media Commission, stated, 'I have often enjoyed the programme but I admit I have sometimes wondered if the jokes go a little near the edge of good taste.' The Rt Revd Charles Henderson, Auxilliary Bishop of Southwark, commented, 'I do not have time to see the show, but I do not object to jokes about the Church. If we can't laugh at ourselves – God help us.'

When an *Evening Standard* reporter phoned the Vatican, a spokesman told him, 'We do not object to jokes about the Roman Catholic Church as long as they are in good taste. People must not be too sensitive about that. We like to think we have a sense of humour.' Allen and his producer Peter Whitmore took the Vatican reply as tacit approval to keep on telling jokes about the clergy. But the parishioners of the north-west weren't so amused. They claimed that Allen made continual attacks on the church. BBC2 'noted' the petition of protest and stated, 'we will look into it'.

The comedian could be forgiven for occasionally jetting off to Australia to forget the whole 'insular business' and people's decided lack of humour. In May 1975, he was in Australia for TV engagements and was again reminded of the broadcast ban that had once been imposed on him. 'I'm not bitter', he told reporters at Sydney airport, obviously annoyed. 'I'm bound to offend some people by telling jokes about God, religion, the Pope, sex. And I send up situations and institutions that are dear to a good many of my audience. But people should realize that when I poke fun at coffins, I'm not ridiculing death.'

He assured some columnists, who persisted in raising the issue of the ban, that viewers had nothing to fear.

'There'll be a lot of chat in my shows,' he said, 'a bit of clowning and a selection of topline guest stars, and maybe a politician or two. The shows will be taped, so there is no problem.'

Away from the studios, he liked to laze bare-chested in the sun by his hotel swimming-pool, munch a sandwich and talk to anyone who cared to listen. To the surprise of some friends, he had eased up considerably on drinking. He admitted that it was no longer one of his favourite hobbies. Most days he sipped tea and reserved the odd beer and glass of champagne for night-time.

For his four shows for the ATN 7 network shows, the comedian was getting $100,000 which placed him above most other entertainers in Australia. His TV pulling power remained enormous, and despite his indiscretions a few years previously, most Australians had forgiven him, even if the media refused to forget.

15   Silver at Montreux

He was on tour with his new one-man stage show, *An Evening with Dave Allen* when the news broke that the BBC had won an award at the Golden Rose TV Festival of Montreux, Switzerland. The second prize of a Silver Rose went to the corporation for the special compilation programme, *Dave Allen at Large*. It came as a disappointment to some delegates who were expecting the first prize of the Golden Rose, but that went to *The Shirley MacLaine Special*, an elaborate spectacular submitted by America's CBS network.

Peter Whitmore, director of *Dave Allen at Large*, travelled to Montreux with his wife Daphne and received the prize on behalf of the comedian. On their return to London, Whitmore telephoned Allen in Eastbourne with the news. 'I told Dave it was a feather in his cap', recalls the director. 'A win at this international festival of light entertainment was regarded as important in television circles and Dave was aware of this. But he is not an emotional man and took the news with typical coolness.'

That weekend Peter and Daphne drove to Eastbourne and arrived at the theatre with about a quarter of an hour to go to the end of the show. Whitmore told the comedian's manager that he had come to show the Silver Rose to Allen and to celebrate the occasion with a few drinks. After a pause, the manager said, 'Why not go on stage at the end of the show and hand the award to him personally?'

'No, I wouldn't do that,' replied the self-effacing Whitmore.

'Why not? I think that Dave would love to see you.'

Whitmore relented and just as the comedian was saying his famous line, 'Good night and may your God go with you', he walked on stage and both men shook hands warmly. Whitmore made a brief speech and handed the Silver Rose to the comedian as the audience applauded. Later, they celebrated the triumph over a bottle of champagne. Whitmore felt no one deserved the award more than Allen who in the past had been nominated several times for BAFTA awards, but failed to get one. The Montreux success was for them both the culmination of years of dedicated work in the comedy series, the most successful of all Allen's TV shows. It had made him an international star.

Sometime previously, in 1976, Stanley Reynolds, the critic of *The Times* had taken stock of Allen, and come to the conclusion that without doubt he was the funniest man working for television. He summed up:

> His humour is odd and rare, but it is an old and time-honoured sort of wit. He is the public-house raconteur. The fellow in the office who disturbs work each morning with his tales about what happened the night before. It is almost impossible to quote him here and at the same time to do justice to his act, because it is the timing and that old cliché about a man being funny not for his jokes but for the way he tells them.
>
> Without pulling funny faces, without comic costumes, simply sitting in a chair, a glass of whisky at his elbow, and a microphone, speaking in a casual everyday manner, Dave Allen is superb.

To Reynolds, the comedian was reminiscent of the American entertainer Bill Cosby. But while Cosby was allowed to sit and chat and be funny, Allen was forced to perform in *those* sketches, and while some of them were very good and the comedian was not a bad character actor, acting was not his gift; his gift was for talk, the tale, the story, the monologue, the Irishman's gift of the gab. Reynolds felt that while Allen did not stoop to having singers and dancers on his show, it would perhaps be a bit more daring and adventurous if the BBC merely let him sit and talk for fifty minutes. It might also prove to be more amusing.

Peter Whitmore disagreed. The sketches, in his view, undoubtedly made *Dave Allen at Large* the phenomenal success it had become. They were loved by studio audiences, and there was no reason to believe that the majority of viewers did not like them. Fifty minutes of chat would be too much and far too predictable. The funny sketches gave the show that unpredictable element viewers found irresistible. Stanley Reynolds was one of the few critics to consider the sketches 'heavy-handed' and sometimes unfunny, but he had ended his review with the words, 'But why quibble with one of the few really funny and watchable spots on television?'

Allen had by now scaled a new peak in his career. People, however, tended to forget that he was also an accomplished TV interviewer and documentary presenter. These programmes released the journalist in him, set his inquisitive mind to work, and brought him face to face with people and issues that otherwise would have escaped his attention as a comedian. At that time, he told Peter Fiddick of the *Guardian*, 'Television is a fascinating business. In some ways it's the poor cousin of theatre and film, but there are great things to be done.'

He saw the potential of TV and wanted to exploit it to the utmost. He did not disguise his ambition. But there was a problem. Having established both his name and face as a comedian, it was hard now to take him seriously as an interviewer. 'In some ways I agree it's hard for me,' he said, 'because if people I'm doing stories about have seen me on television and don't like me they're more inclined to think I'm there to make fun of them. On the other hand, if they've liked me as a comedian, then they're more inclined to unbend and tell me the stories.'

As a documentary-maker, he wore a different hat. Once, he went to New York to make a documentary about the emigrant Irish, but discovered that they had become so well assimilated, except on St Patrick's Day, that there really wasn't a story. He ended up making a programme about the city itself called *In the Melting Pot*. On his return to Britain he made another documentary about English black people living around Cardiff and afterwards felt it was a mistake. As he recalled, 'I think it would have worked better as a debate rather than a film.'

Just now he was fully preoccupied with his one-man show, *An Evening with Dave Allen*. It was a two-and-a-half-hour show without script, prompter, notes or other aids. This approach puzzled newspaper columnists who came to see him and wondered how he remembered all the stories and jokes. The comedian assured them he prepared all his own material. Like most comedians he possesses the kind of brain that stores jokes away, but his memory was nothing phenomenal otherwise. He didn't rehearse jokes or routines, not even when he was on TV, but he did sit down quietly and work a joke through his head.

Even though he used the minimum of stage props for his stage show, people wondered why, for instance, the stool was there. Adopting this style wasn't deliberate, he says, nor was it contrived. He did not consider himself a deliberate person, planning years ahead. The stool was there because he got tired of standing up, and, with everyone out in the audience having a drink, he thought he might as well have one.

It was Irish-born Dick Condon who invited him to present his solo show in Norwich in March 1978. Condon was the successful manager of the local Theatre Royal and although they had never met, he had unbounded admiration for the comedian and regularly followed his TV shows. 'Dave has this unique ability to entertain', he says today. 'It would be difficult to describe him as anything other than a funny man. His comedy sketches I consider to be excellent, well worked out and in no way predictable, mainly because they were either fresh material or reworked older sketches with a completely new twist.'

He had no apprehension about booking Allen for the Theatre Royal, and was convinced his humour would not be hard to sell in Norwich; in fact, within a matter of hours of the box-office opening nearly all the tickets were sold. It hadn't always been that way for comedians in Norwich. In the 1950s and 60s it was regarded as the comedians' graveyard, something of a theatrical backwater before the resurgence of the Theatre Royal in the early 70s. Morecambe and Wise, for instance, had died a death on the Theatre Royal stage in the 60s, but later returned to score some great successes.

Condon and Allen quickly became friends. To the theatre manager, he was a sensitive person, highly intelligent, a good judge of character, observant and with a talent which was so wide-ranging that he began to consider him unique. They were both night people, in so far as they liked to chat over a meal and a drink into early morning. Condon found that the comedian liked to speak his own poetry.

On that first night, Allen walked from the Maids Head where he was staying to the theatre, entered casually by the stage door and proceeded to prepare for the show. He exchanged a few friendly words with stage manager Jack Bowhill and sipped a glass of champagne. To Condon, he did not appear in any way nervous before the rise of the curtain; if anything, he gave the impression of being cool and casual in his approach. Soon the Theatre Royal audience acclaimed him.

'Norwich audiences took to Dave Allen like a duck to water', remembered Condon. 'His story-telling approach was exactly right for the largely rural audience. The quick-fire comics are much less an attraction in Norwich. The pace of life here is slower and very akin to Irish life.' After the final curtain, when the manager visited the comedian in his dressing-room to congratulate him, he found that, like most performers at the end of a show, he was on a high, but it was on a contained level. In Allen's case, the most natural response was to seek company, friendship, good food and a glass of wine which helped the gentle restoration to reality.

Allen's visit to Norwich set up a new box-office record for the Theatre Royal, when £21,876 was taken for his six sell-out performances. Every night it was the same, recalls Condon. The comedian had the audience eating out of his hand right from the moment he walked on stage, said, 'Good Evening' to a group of people sitting stage right, got a gentle response, walked to stage left, and in a louder and more firm voice proclaimed his greeting of 'Good Evening' to those sitting on that side. Their response was much louder; then the comedian announced that he had found the Roman Catholics in the audience, and proceeded to give them his blessing. The audience rocked with laughter.

After each night's show, Condon and the comedian dined together and talked endlessly about art and the theatre. Condon found that he could relax in Allen's company and, like Ken Dodd, another entertainer who took Norwich by storm, he was articulate and a good conversationalist. To ensure that he had sufficient champagne during his stay in Norwich, the manager had bottles delivered from a local wine company.

As he toured *An Evening with Dave Allen*, the comedian was often asked about politics, because he was considered a thoughtful person who appeared to be perceptive about a lot of different matters. In his view, it was understandable and he tried to answer the questions truthfully. At that time, he reckoned that the leaders in Britain and world politics were too grey to find a response in the audience, compared with Khrushchev, the first Wilson government, even Gaitskell in opposition. Politics, he was inclined to think, was too much to devote to an entire show. As he told *Guardian* man Peter Fiddick, 'I wouldn't want to hear myself talking just about politics for that long. You can poke, you can dig, but in the end it would be too serious for the audience – their laughter would leave them.'

To Allen, it was simply not a good subject. 'You would have to go for all sides, find things against everyone. Your platform, then, is cynicism.' He made no secret of his preference for subjects such as religion, sex, papal infallibility, cemeteries, madness and nose-picking, though not necessarily in that order. He put it another way. He was, he said, eternally grateful for three things – religion, madness and rules. If there weren't those things in life, he'd have nothing to talk about. He'd have to be a mime artist. A lot of comedy came from being irked by something like blinkered thinking or the stupidity of bureaucracy.

He saw comedy as a mirror held up to life which gave back a cock-eyed reflection. That was why comedy could sometimes be uncomfortable, because the mirror showed you yourself as you really were. In any conversation with the comedian, fun was never far away from the surface.

Despite his eagerness for laying bare the foibles of other people, he was still intensely protective about his private life. Curiously, he thought it extraordinary that the media wanted to know about his personal life, and his reasoning did not always make sense. 'If I go to a doctor, I'm not interested if he's a homosexual or dresses up in drag or beats his wife', he explained. 'I'm only interested in his professional competence. I protect my private life because it is private and nobody else's business. I don't mind people knowing I've got a wife and children. That's fine. But I draw the line at that.'

None the less, there were a lot of people in audiences around Britain who were eager to learn more about Judith Stott, actress and mother, and his children. Obviously the information would not be forthcoming from the comedian.

16 The Boston Verdict

'He could be a movie star', said actor Robert Stephens. 'He is the same type of actor as the Hollywood greats like Clark Gable, Humphrey Bogart or Gary Cooper. They never actually step outside themselves, they make the part them.'

On the face of it, it seemed a wild exaggeration, yet producer Ernest Maxin had said more or less the same thing years before when he thought that Allen should have concentrated on movies because he possessed the requisite charm for romantic roles.

Producer Peter Whitmore did not quite agree. He felt that Allen's forte was comedy alone and his dead-pan style was eminently suited to his story-telling. Dick Condon was of the same mind, although he was impressed by the comedian's versatility. Stephens had just played with Allen in Alan Bennett's play *One Fine Day* on ITV and in the critics' view, acquitted himself admirably in the part of George Philips, head of a commercial property department. They had first met fifteen years before at Chichester when Stephens was in a play with Albert Finney and the comic came backstage to see him. 'I remember Dave sat on the floor drinking a bottle of Guinness. I'd heard nothing about him at all then.'

Allen was surprised by Stephens' fulsome praise, for usually actors' comments about each other were not fit for human ears. But the actor was sincere, and was to add, 'Dave addresses the camera and makes the audience happy to watch him. It's not like playing Hamlet or King Lear, then you have to step inside yourself and build the character. It's the difference between why Olivier was not a great *film* star and why his wife Vivien Leigh was. I was delighted to play opposite Dave. He did the part like himself, take it or leave it. I thought he used his baleful individual personality very well and it suited the character.'

Stephens, the star of movies such as *The Prime of Miss Jean Brodie* and *The Private Life of Sherlock Holmes*, regarded himself basically as a stage actor who had to create a part. In *One Fine Day* he played Welby, a smooth-talking boss of a large London firm of estate agents. Bennett, whose plays had become extremely popular at that time with television audiences, was impressed enough with Allen's perform- ance to remark, 'Dave interpreted the part of Philips as I wrote it and his concentration never waned.'

It was the comedian's first straight role on TV and he admitted he was satisfied with his own performance. Taking the role meant that his earnings had dropped appreciably, but money wasn't everything to him. He was eager to stretch himself in acting terms and was prepared to consider more drama if the right role came along. At forty-three, he had now done almost everything except play a Shakespearean part as Ken Dodd and Frankie Howerd had done. Others wondered if he had let the opportunity to be a film star pass him by. He was no longer in the full bloom of youth for romantic screen roles and he wasn't actually unduly exerting himself to get into films. He was more concerned with touring his one-man show, *An Evening with Dave Allen* and it was proving a big attraction in theatres all over Britain.

He still found time to do his television shows, but in this respect his attitude to his children seeing him on the box was puzzling. It was a case of 'Not in front of the children'. His daughter Jane, son Edward and stepson Jonathan were packed off to bed because their father did not want TV to interfere with their bedtimes. Another reason he gave was that he did not want them affected by his life story or his career. One of the few shows the children saw him do was *Peter Pan*, and that was a matinée performance.

Soon his thoughts were turned to Australia. Hardly a year passed without a tour or TV work down under.

Usually he worked a hectic schedule as he made shows for Channel Nine. Although he sometimes brought his own producer Austin Steele from England, he himself was very much acting the executive producer. He watched the shooting of every skit carefully, and quietly, courteously, made suggestions for changes in shots, action and the script itself. His requests were always agreed to by everybody concerned. During the shooting, he put a complete ban on interviews. Those around him sometimes thought he looked exhausted, but he shrugged off such suggestions. 'I'm not tired,' he would say, with a grin, as he carefully examined his reflection in his dressing-room mirror. Suddenly he would laugh and remark to those nearby, 'I'm a work dog. I enjoy it.'

Australians were occasionally curious about why he kept coming back, particularly since he was a big star in Britain and did not need work elsewhere. The comedian was frank, 'I come back because I have some very good friends here, because it's a good market. For enjoyment, I suppose, and the sheer pleasure. It's a nice way of earning your living, seeing the world.' He ate little as he worked, reserving that pleasure, like good conversation, for night time. He continued to smoke a French brand of cigarettes and drank a lot of tea. After the day's shooting was completed, he watched the previous day's rushes critically. It was 8.30, often later, before he and his producer, Austin Steele, got back to their hotel where, over a meal, they discussed the next day's shooting and scripts. Then, it was bed.

As a close observer of humour, the comedian now thought that it got harder. In the 1960s gags in Britain were about Profumo and Mandy Rice-Davis. In the late 70s, humour had become deeper, more searching. As Allen said, 'Comedians talking about politicians now are more intellectually aware – the audience is more aware – so it has to be harder.' Yet he had refrained from poking fun at certain things, like people who stuttered or with mental disorders. He avoided what was then called 'Paki-bashing'. His own brand of comedy was uncomplicated – he simply looked for the ridiculous in life. For instance, he saw people in lifts as funny or people looking for a parking space in London, and he never tired of seeing the fun in telephones and how people used them.

America, because of its size, held a great fascination for the comedian. He had gone there to make documentaries and found it a good place to put the spotlight on people and their eccentricities. Now, as May 1981 approached, he was seriously thinking of going there with his solo show, *An Evening with Dave Allen*. He chose Boston as a kind of tryout before he would make his Broadway début. He was aware that few British comedians had made it in America, and this surprised him, and also inspired him to have a go himself.

That May afternoon, he met members of the Boston press in a downtown restaurant and talked to them about his show and about comedy in general. He also screened videotapes of what the press was to call 'his zanyness'. His name was not entirely unknown in the States. The *Dave Allen at Large* series was shown on Channel 38 and the critics had commented favourably on the funny sketches. One woman columnist now asked him if he had singled out the Catholic Church as the butt of his sometimes ribald sketches. Almost casually, the comedian replied, 'An Irishman in London had complained that I had blasphemed the Pope in one of my shows and I told him if he knew anything about the costume worn by the actor portraying the prelate in the sketch, he would have discovered that it was the garb of the High Church of England.'

He said that he had a lot of religious people writing to him about that particular programme, but less than ten of them had failed to see the fun in it. It was the lay people who assumed that the Church didn't have a sense of humour. There was a giggle among the press present when he added, with a grin, 'I know a whole convent of nuns who wrote to me that they always sneak out at night to watch the show and sometimes they supply me with good material, too – not to be used, of course, but nice material.'

He disclosed that he had never joined a religious organization, although at the age of fourteen, he had taken a non-drinking pledge which he kept, but not for long. He assured his listeners that he avoided going for the 'cheap laugh' at the expense of handicapped people. 'I also tend to stay away from racist remarks.' He said that the content of his stage show would be different from his TV series and all he needed, besides his skills, were a stool and a glass of water, and he would be discussing 'universal matters'. 'We're all hung up with things like insurance, mortgages, wives, children, bureaucrats and so forth. The show's material should vary as much as thirty per cent night to night. I'll talk to the audience and discuss a series of subjects, and hope to make them amusing.'

He said he liked the immediacy of reaction he got from a theatre audience because one knew on the spot if one's material was effective or not. He was quizzed about the David Frost episode of a few years before when he turned down the opportunity to fill Frost's slot on TV. He emphasized that it would have meant being on camera four days a week for forty-two weeks and he vetoed the assignment as being too arduous. Asked about appearing with the Beatles, he said, 'They gradually took over as stars of the show. They were very dynamic and even at that early date I saw something special in them.'

Kevin Kelly, a staffer on the *Boston Globe*, says today that before Broadway began its modern theatre previews Boston had often been used as a tryout venue by companies and individual comedians. It was a city with a rich theatrical tradition and most of the 'greats' had played there from time to time. Kelly – a Canadian – in his capacity as theatre critic, had visited Britain, Ireland and the Continent, and had a good knowledge of international playwrights and actors. On Tuesday, 13 May, he went along to the Wilbur Theater to write about *An Evening with Dave Allen*, which was described as 'a programme of comedy in two acts'. Next day he told the readers of the *Boston Globe*:

> A little of Dave Allen goes a long way, which may be one of the principal reasons the BBC comedian earned an

American following from a limited time-slot on late night television.

Alone on stage, propped up only by a glass of liquor in the first act and, in the second act, four glasses of champagne (one of which he gives away), Allen leans his left elbow on the mike stand while talking into the mouthpiece he holds in his right hand. Most of the time he stares at the floor. Occasionally he advances to the lip of the stage and talks directly to the audience, sometimes inveigling a hapless onlooker into what turns out to be an embarrassing exchange (for the onlooker, that is). The pattern doesn't have much pace. The humour tends to be bleak, offensive, circular, cold and rather unpleasant. Within all that, the humour is sometimes brilliant. There is, for example, his truly unsettling (I almost said Swiftian) flight of fancy involving the pent-up energy the universe would gain from making love rather than war. Allen's targets are diverse, yet – except for an odd reach of far-out fantasy – often limited in development. Despite the ease of his offhand style (he really seems to be thinking out the material as he says it), his satiric sense is essentially deadbeat. It frequently plays dismal. It winds up disheartening instead of provocative which is, perhaps, the distinction between a genuine 'Thinking Man's Comic' and 'Clever Comedian'. Whatever else, Dave Allen is on stage far too long. He really belongs to the tube, or in a club interspersed with other acts. For all his savage logic, he's finally found wanting.

The most telling word in Kelly's review was 'bleak', and today, nearly ten years after he wrote it, he stands over it. Americans, in his opinion, prefer the Bob Hope style which comes across with effervescence and optimism. And they don't like comedians going on interminably unless they see them as uniquely funny like the late Jimmy Durante or Jack Benny. Kelly felt that Allen's exploratory style of humour and his harping on about the human condition tended to irk, even bore, some Americans who didn't want to be reminded of their own failings and vices.

For Allen, it was a useful tryout before he decided on a Broadway date. He could expect a more cosmopolitan audience in New York, but even then critic Kevin Kelly wasn't entirely confident that the comedian would be a success there. Allen was more confident and before he left Boston expressed an eagerness to play Broadway. He would, he told himself, never be happy unless he met this greatest of all challenges for a comedian.

17   Broadway Début

New York in the fall. Always a salubrious time for a visit to this most cosmopolitan of America's cities, and Allen confidently chose that September of 1981 to make his Broadway début. Undeniably, his solo show, *An Evening with Dave Allen* would be facing stiff competition, for the Broadway scene was dominated by classy musicals and plays, including Tennessee Williams's latest, *Something Cloudy, Something Clear*.

Among the popular musicals were *Chorus Line*, *Annie* and *42nd Street*, and the most talked of plays were *Children of a Lesser God* and *Amadeus*, both of which featured in the Tony Awards. In a lighter vein, Paul Simon and Art Garfunkel were expected to attract half a million people to their free charity concert on the Great Lawn of Central Park and already it was billed as the musical event of the year. At the same time, legendary entertainer Danny Kaye was quietly preparing to mount the podium to conduct the New York Philharmonic Orchestra.

Allen would be arriving in a New York not greatly changed, if one was to judge by the newspapers. Screamed a headline in the *Post*: 'SENATE CONTENDER IS MUGGED ON SUBWAY'; and other reports highlighted Mafia revenge shootings, violence in Harlem, and a spate of armed robberies. Despite the rise in crime and social disorder, Broadway seemed to be unaffected and continued on its merry way with the usual first-nighters going to Sardi's after the show, where playwrights and actors nervously awaited the verdicts of the 'Butchers of Broadway'.

Where comedians and clowns were concerned,

Broadway could claim a glorious tradition, extending back to the Golden Era of the 1920s and funny men like Joe Cook, Jimmy Durante, W.C.Fields and Ed Wynn, and later when Bob Hope, Jack Benny, the Marx Brothers, and Danny Kaye sent gleeful audiences into the streets to catch late-night transport. The name Dave Allen did not mean much to Americans; to most of them there was only one Allen and that was Woody Allen, although Steve Allen was also a prominent name in show-business.

In American terms, Dave Allen had only gained syndicated TV exposure in New York, so he was opening on Broadway at a distinct disadvantage. A comedian with a big TV or movie following stood a better chance of packing a theatre. Furthermore, the history of overseas comedians on Broadway did not augur well; the more recent failure of the exuberant Bruce Forsyth, who had arrived with millionaire backing, was certainly not forgotten. Yet, Allen did not seem in any way overawed by the prospect before him and was very keen to get on with his one-man show at the famous Booth Theatre on 45th Street.

The Dublin-born funny man would occupy the same dressing-room as fellow Irish actor, Donal Donnelly, when he starred in *The Elephant Man* for two years on Broadway. Donnelly was looking forward to Allen's visit as he was a great fan of his, but they were also friends from their London days; their little daughters went to the same school, and sometimes they met to talk about the theatre and would be joined by actor T.P.McKenna, another Irish friend of Allen's.

Donnelly, dark-haired and stocky, had made his Broadway début years before in Brian Friel's play, *Philadelphia, Here I Come*, and today remembers that début vividly: 'The opening night on Broadway was scarifying. The fear of the unknown seized us. When we asked anybody beforehand how they thought the play would do, they would answer, "Oh, gee, I dunno." You must not be associated with a forecast on Broadway in case you forecast wrongly.'

To Donnelly, a thoughtful man of the theatre, Allen had

talent to burn. 'To me, he was simply brilliant', he recalls. 'His gift was in his mischievous story-telling, the way he held his audience, his superb timing and delivery of the punchline. I used to watch his TV shows and laugh openly in my room. His appeal to audiences, whether on TV, in the theatre or nightclub was immediate. I thought, though, he might have considered a Broadway visit earlier in his career.'

There was something else that slightly worried Donnelly, and it was whether Broadway was in fact the right place for *An Evening with Dave Allen*. He kept asking himself if off-Broadway would not be a better choice. It was more intimate, less daunting, and Allen might stand a better chance of packing the theatre for his five weeks' run. Nonetheless, he was delighted that the comedian had at last made his decision to play Broadway, if only to show Americans his unique talent.

Allen's TV shows had also attracted New York theatre critic Clive Barnes and he was looking forward to his visit to the Booth Theatre. 'Something about his individual style intrigued me,' recalls Barnes. 'I wondered if New Yorkers would take to his story-telling.'

Allen's show was billed as an evening of 'humour and wit' and in the *Going Out Guide* in the *New York Times* he was said to have 'appeared on TV and in a theatre in Boston'. Mention was made of the TV series, *Dave Allen at Large*, in which he was described as the link between a series of skits performed by himself and his company. John J. O'Connor, the *New York Times* television critic was quoted as saying, 'There are jokes, among other things, the Australians, the Irish, the English, religion and infidelity. Some may be found insulting, but Mr Allen's ingratiating manner can make the outrageous surprisingly acceptable.'

It was noticeable in press interviews that Allen was quick to correct columnists who described him as 'a British or English funny man'. He stressed his Dublin upbringing and his subsequent struggle to make comedy his career. In this respect, he told Patricia O'Haire of the *Daily News*, 'I never thought I'd make it my life's work, however, until I got the taste of it at a Butlin's Holiday Camp where I was a Red Coat. The taste stayed with me.' Miss O'Haire admitted that she was 'a Dave Allen freak' and wrote that she had fallen into the habit a year before of watching Benny Hill on TV in New York and the programme that followed him, which was *Dave Allen at Large*, and now looked forward to seeing, as she said, Mr Allen on stage. She advised her readers not to miss this 'great opportunity'.

She regarded Allen as a very funny man, although she said she could not prove it in print as she had no Allen one-liners to quote, as was the case when writing about Bob Hope or Henry Youngman; no sight gags to remember, as with Benny Hill, no routine like Jack Benny. She saw Allen basically as a story-teller who built up his stories as carefully as the Turner Construction Company built theirs. In conversation with the entertainer, she found he had 'kicked the habit of smoking' and the comedian explained why: 'I just got angry having to pay almost a pound for a packet. So, about two months ago, I decided to stop. I was in an airport, and I walked up to a fellow who was lighting up and gave him all I had. He took them, too, when I told him I was finished.'

In New York he was regarded as 'handsome', and one woman columnist remarked on his 'curly black hair showing a bit of grey'; he was being profiled as a nice guy from Ireland and newspaper columnists were intrigued by his stories about his Red Coat days, which he never tired of describing as his 'apprenticeship'.

Miss O'Haire of the *Daily News* had grown to like the comedian and ended off her piece in the paper, 'What's Dave Allen doing in New York is still telling stories, but the material will be new, with probably different stories from night to night. It would be nice to have something to laugh at on Broadway for a change.'

Despite the welter of news in New York papers that September, coverage of Allen's show was extensive. Clive Barnes in the *Post* wrote one of the most favourable reviews of the season which was headed, 'IT'S DAVID

THE KILLER COMIC'. The critic went on to say that the season, which had taken so long to get going, had actually got going last night at the Booth Theater with a one-man show, *An Evening with Dave Allen*. But he warned his readers, 'It would depend somewhat on your sense of humour – particularly as to how you regard irreverent and, I suppose the word is explicit, satire about sex, bodily functions and religion in general, and the Roman Catholic faith in particular.'

Barnes admitted that he found the comedian absolutely hilarious, positively one of the original comedians in the world today. Great. And the show was done on a bare stage, well, nearly. In fact, a stool on which there was a spotlit glass of an amber, effervescent liquid, and a microphone. An amiable man in strange-looking dinner jacket, appearing like an urbane and intellectualized leprechaun wandered on and the new Broadway season was up and ambling. It was, however, when the critic explored deeper that his review became even more interesting:

> Beneath his suave off-hand and slightly alcoholic image – although on stage Allen appears to be a sipper rather than a drinker – lies a killer comedian. His style is also remarkable. Imagine, those of you who are aficianados of the stand-up comic, a style that embraces George Carlin, Lenny Bruce, David Brenner, disconcertingly adds Bob Hope, and then goes beyond the fringe in a British accent. Yet despite this seeming mishmash it is all pure Dave Allen.

During the show, the comedian wanders around the stage and chats to the audience. At times, Barnes thought that he wandered too much, at least from his subject. However, he found most of Allen's material 'fresh and original' and he was struck by his 'off-beat charm, wicked sense of mockery, and acute sense of the ridiculous'. And his meandering stream of consciousness, which always seemed to meander in the right direction, would almost preclude other writers, except that for the purveyors of the

odd, crisp one-liner. In Barnes's view, Allen was
essentially a comedian of attitude. He thought that a lot of
his comedy derived from the comedian's Irish-Catholic
upbringing, although he triumphantly proclaims in the
show, 'I'm an atheist, thank God'; while you can take Mr
Allen out of the Catholic Church, you quite clearly cannot
take the Catholic Church out of Mr Allen. The critic
summed up:

> His careful retelling of a Catholic childhood, and his
> devastating demolition of Bible stories from the Garden of
> Eden onwards, shows us as much affection as it does
> disgust. You sense that he is a Catholic dropout wearing a
> parachute. Not that the Church is his only target. He is
> great on logic – comparing with convulsively funny
> examples differences between vertical thinking, which is
> logic, and lateral thinking, which appears to be Ireland.
> 'Ireland,' he tells us, 'is the only place in the world where
> procrastination takes on a sense of urgency.'

Allen could not have hoped for a better review. Clive
Barnes was influential and the fact that he described the
comedian as 'a cult hero' underlined the admiration he
had for him. But could one favourable review sway the
masses? As it proved, other critics were less kind. The
redoubtable Frank Rich in the *New York Times* gave no
warning in his introductory lines to his review of what he
really felt about *An Evening with Dave Allen*. In those
opening lines he described the comedian as 'a most
appealing fellow' and though at the brink of middle age
still possessed that innocent mischievousness of an errant
choirboy about him; he didn't have to work at being cute.
Indeed, he successfully created the illusion that he wasn't
working at all. As Rich put it, 'Mr Allen looks so
comfortable and relaxed that the audience can't help but
feel at home, too.'

The critic admired the comedian's poise, and he also felt
he should be saluted for his bravery, as he was far less
familiar to TV audiences in New York than either Woody
or Steve Allen. Yet he was here, offering his one-man

show. To Rich, Allen's gambit did not pay off. Although he had skills to go with his ingratiating personality – most notably a highly professional sense of timing – his material was rarely, if ever, worthy of the crisp delivery it received. By present-day standards – whether those of Monty Python or Johnny Carson – his comic ramblings seemed tame and tired. If jokes were music, he wrote, Dave Allen's would be Mantovani. His satirical targets were all too familiar: sexual hypocrisies, television commercials, changing attitudes in social behaviour. Faithful to his Irish roots, he also took a slightly naughty attitude towards the Church and devoted much of his act (too much) to a cock-eyed recital of the tall tales in the Old Testament. While Mr Allen was not afraid to use four-letter words, describe bodily functions or mock the clergy, his comedy always remained resolutely inoffensive. "The act of love is how we all got here," he says, almost as if to apologize, during one of his more ribald spiels. At such times it was hard to tell whether he wanted the audience to laugh or chant amen.' Rich summed up:

> Because Mr Allen's game is to spot the 'illogical' aspects of life, one does keep hoping that his easy-going trains of thought will ascend to some higher plateau of insight or wit. When he fails to move beyond the mildly illogical to the truly absurd, one wonders if his years in television have homogenized his seemingly flinty Irish soul. Whatever the explanation, tedium sets in – and so does the suspicion that a half-hour routine has been needlessly stretched to the length of a Broadway show. No doubt this pleasant performer is fun in short takes on the tube or in a nightclub, but, as the star of an evening of theatre, Dave Allen is decidedly miscast.

Nor did Douglas Watt in the *Daily News* pull any punches. Under the heading, 'DAVE ALLEN: FRESH MATERIAL COULD HELP', and accompanied by a smiling picture of the comedian, Watt was emphatic:

> Chop off an hour, give him a good editor and perhaps a writing staff (I assume he provides his own material) and put him on a nightclub floor, and Dave Allen the British

humourist who last night began a five-week stand at the
Booth Theater might prove irresistible. As things stand,
he's far from that.

However, the critic found the comedian's Bible stories
sharp and nicely timed, if somewhat broad and
superficial. Too much of the first half of his long
programme, he said, was devoted to scatological jokes,
and rude comments on the human anatomy and various
bodily functions. Watt's summing up was particularly
caustic:

> Opening a new Broadway season (new if, like me you
> count Labour Day as the kickoff date) Allen seems like
> small beer. Bored with his first hour, I'd gladly have left at
> intermission. But then I'd have missed his tangle with the
> Scripture. That's funny enough, on the whole, but too
> often Allen put me in mind of the ill-fated comedian in
> Lenny Bruce's classic, 'Comic at the Palladium' routine.

Watt's was unquestionably a damning review and
hardly the sort to attract fickle New Yorkers to the Booth
Theater. Much now depended on Walter Kerr's review in
the Sunday issue of the *New York Times*. If he found the
show mediocre, then Allen's début on Broadway would be
far from a memorable one.

That Sunday, 27 September, the headline: over Walter
Kerr's review in the *New York Times* boded no good at all
for Allen's one-man show. 'A COMIC AT A LOSS'
instantly suggested that one of the city's most experienced
and influential theatre critics was neither impressed nor
stimulated by *An Evening with Dave Allen*. The second
paragraph of his review read:

> I liked Dave Allen less and less the more I heard of him,
> and for quite a long while I just couldn't say why. For
> instance, I found myself chuckling in spite of myself fairly
> often during the earlier sashays into rambling verbal
> nonsense. Though Mr Allen's accent and experience are
> mainly British, he was born in Dublin, and he's still cosily
> flippant with an Irish joke. Leaning on his microphone

stand as though it were the well-rubbed frontage of a pub bar, he has no difficulty tracing Irish contrariness to a love of the literal. Watching a funeral go by and asking 'Who's dead?' he gets the straight-faced reply, 'The one in the box'.

Although he confessed he wasn't elated by the comedian's references to sex, urination, nose-picking and TV commercials, Kerr was still puzzled by the fact that half-way through the show he was still chuckling. He concluded that it was Allen's exasperation that was amusing him. As he explained,

> Mr Allen is not content to let things be as they are, whether among fish or people. He is appalled, outraged, given to highest dudgeon over the preposterous taboos we so placidly accept, over the no-nos we docilely submit to from church, state and mama's toilet training. And outrage boiling over is always at least half-way funny. Isn't it? Well, up to a point it is. After a while one does feel hectored.

Donal Donnelly brought his two young sons, Damian and Jonathan along to see the show. Afterwards, the actor went backstage to introduce the boys to Allen and it was a happy reunion scene in the star's dressing-room. 'They were simply crazy about Dave's humour,' recalls Donnelly, 'and he shook their hands and talked about his London days.'

Privately, Donnelly was unhappy about certain aspects of the show. He felt that the comedian had dwelt too long on the Old Testament and he suspected the lengthy monologue tended to bore the audience. The result was that New Yorkers never really got to know Dave Allen, the mischievous story-teller. 'I think the audience would have loved half a dozen more good stories instead of all this Old Testament stuff', Donnelly says today, almost ten years after Allen's Broadway début.

He knew that Allen could have made a bigger impact and that he hadn't upset him. He was inclined to believe that an off-Broadway setting would have served his humour better, and given more impact to his gags and stories. Whether the engagement of an American to direct the show would have improved it will never be known, though Donnelly believes that Allen could have been better advised on his Broadway choice of material. New Yorkers simply did not get enough of his funny stories. To Donnelly, Dave Allen had not made the most of his big opportunity in America.

Clive Barnes says he is still surprised, even puzzled, by the failure of the comedian to make it on Broadway. He himself had given him the most favourable review and today stands by every word. As he said,

> I enjoyed the show and considered Dave Allen one of the best comedians in the world at the time. He is truly an original. Maybe American tastes are different to British tastes and for that reason Americans did not take to him in big enough numbers to make his show a success. But then it is also true that Irish and British comics have never done particularly well on Broadway and that, too, is an important factor. It still amazes me though that Dave Allen did not find a more warm response.

Undeterred by his Broadway experiences, Allen returned to Britain to continue his tour of *An Evening with Dave Allen*; at least he could be assured of packed theatres and enthusiastic audiences. It was proving his most successful stage show ever and he had not finished with his tour by any means. That November he brought it to London's Haymarket Theatre and the reviews were reasonably good. Eric Shorter in the *Daily Telegraph*, under the heading 'HUMOUR, ROBUST AND NAÏVE', said simply that 'Dave Allen, irreverent as ever, is back in London with his microphone (too loud), his stool (never sat upon) and his robustly naïve humour.

Unlike the New York critics, Shorter was not put off by Allen's sly references to either the Old or New Testaments, nor his forays into sexual innuendo and TV commercials. But the closing lines of his review supplied food for thought:

Dave Allen may have been called the Thinking Man's comedian. In fact he simply expresses uninhibitedly most of a thinking man's inhibitions. And by saying what is normally left unspoken, he releases our shame and our laughter. But after an hour or so (and he went on for nearly three hours before I had to depart) there is a monotony in the style of his joking.

18   Rumours of a Rift

Maple Croft, the Allens' home near Henley-on-Thames, had seven bedrooms, a swimming-pool, and a walled herb garden. It stood on nearly nine acres, much of it wooded. Newspapers described it as the comedian's mansion, his status symbol. To visitors it was an ideal retreat for the peripatetic Allen. But in that February of 1982 it was not an entirely happy place.

Friends close to the Allens feared there was a strain in their marriage, and that it was fraught with domestic difficulties. Already, in show-business circles, it was rumoured that there was a rift between the couple and this seemed to be confirmed when papers tried to verify the story. The Allens' housekeeper, who lived in a lodge at the entrance of the half-hidden drive, said they had not been together at the house for some time, though the Allens still visited the place separately.

Puzzled by the flow of enquiries, she said she had last seen 'Mr Allen at the house some days before and that Judith would be away in London for some days'. The comedian's secretary, Maria Degeler and his personal manager Tony Hayes refused to discuss the Allen marriage. Ms Degeler intimated it would not be possible to talk to the comedian about it. 'I thought that's what you phoned about', Hayes replied to further newspaper enquiries, and added, 'I don't think you'll get any reaction from anyone – it's as awkward for you as it is for me.'

Throughout his eighteen years married to Judith Stott, Allen never once discussed their marriage nor his own private affairs, so it was understandable that a wall of silence should now encircle Maple Croft. With Judith anxious to protect their three children from the rumours, experienced Fleet Street gossip-writers knew that the story would be almost impossible to crack. Undoubtedly, news of the rift came as a complete surprise to most people, for the Allens' marriage, as far as they knew, appeared to be working and it looked as if they had made it against the odds. Judith had provided a solid base for her husband and as a family they were happy and secure. However, in the ensuing weeks and months the speculation grew and Judith made no secret of their split. The house was put on the market for £325,000. The full realization of the break-up dawned on her as she began to show would-be purchasers round the house – the house she had come to accept as her permanent home. They were bleak days in her life and close friends knew she was both embittered and saddened by events.

Yet the break-up seemed a familiar story, something that was almost expected to happen in show-business relationships. As far as people knew, it was not the case of *that* other woman; the difficulties arose because the marriage had failed to work on its own terms. True, as in any other marriages, there had been domestic dis-agreements, but Judith was always determined to cover up the cracks for the sake of the children and keep Maple Croft their home. Now she had to admit that their marriage had irretrievably broken down and that they had reached a stage of non-communication. Soon the lawyers would be called in to sort out the divorce proceedings.

For Judith, it was a shattering business. Remembering their whirlwind romance in Australia, marriage after only a few months of courtship and Dave's determination to join her in England even at the expense of his lucrative TV work in Sydney, made the break-up seem all the more absurd and inexplicable. For the first time, she felt hurt, even vulnerable. Despite the support of her close friends, she hardly knew where to turn. At fifty, it wasn't easy to resume her stage and screen career, yet friends urged her to do so as swiftly as possible, assuring her that it was the only way for her to forget the present trauma.

Neither was it a happy time for the comedian. Besides

the trauma of his marriage break-up, he had other things on his mind. His brother John had a serious alcoholic problem, and unless treated properly would probably die. As brothers they had remained close, although from time to time they lost touch, yet Allen never quite forgot his older brother. Had not John first encouraged him to become a professional comedian? Allen discussed the problem with his brother Peter in Dublin, and it was decided to pay for expert treatment for John. 'I am determined to do everything to help my brother', Allen confided in friends. It wasn't going to be easy, for John, outgoing and jovial, had always been fond of a drink and was considered the best of company.

Despite his anxieties, Allen continued to tour with his one-man show. It was proving lucrative and his popularity had not apparently diminished. He was still able to pack theatres up and down the country. In Liverpool, he invariably played one-night stands because of the difficulty of finding a suitable theatre. 'I think it was a pity', recalls Philip Key of the Liverpool *Daily Post*. 'Dave commanded a large following in the city and his show could have run for at least a full week at a time in a big theatre.'

Key, a Londoner who had comfortably settled in Liverpool, enjoyed comedians and counted among his friends Ken Dodd and Tom O'Connor. He found that Allen appealed to Merseysiders and attributed this to the city's Catholic background. People did not mind his swipes at the Church, in fact they considered his stories very funny. As Key explained, 'They enjoyed them as long as Dave didn't lapse into bad taste. Merseysiders are good listeners and there was always complete silence as he told his long stories and audiences laughed loudly at his punchlines.'

Off-stage, both men got on well and enjoyed a chat. To Key, Allen was a very funny man, a particularly smooth performer. He was a star who was in complete command of the stage. In Liverpool, he gagged about the missing section of his index finger on his left hand. Key found it was a topic that seemed to fascinate people. As Allen said, 'People come up to me in the street and ask if I'm Dave Allen. When I say I am they reply, "Are you sure? Show us your hand"'. Key had discovered that most comedians kept a file of sketches and gags at home and expressed surprise when the comedian admitted he never had done so. 'Most of them are in my head, which burns with ideas, some a little too rich for television.' Allen was a great admirer of old-time comics like Buster Keaton and Harold Langdon, and he particularly liked the Keaton film in which rocks come tumbling down on him from a hill. Buster avoids them all – apart from the last small one that hits him on the ankle.

Allen liked to add, 'If we were doing that for TV I would need eighty-five fellows with thirty-five rocks each to throw down. They would tot it up forty pounds for each man, sixty pounds for each costume and that would be the end of it.' He did, however, once do a television sketch which lasted just a few seconds and involved ninety-three men and a telephone box. The whole sketch cost about £10,000. It was a funny sketch, but he didn't know whether it was actually worth the money.

In conversation with the comedian, Philip Key found him to be 'a serious chap', with a deep concern about many of the world's ills. He was sickened, for example, by the political system in South Africa – 'I couldn't believe I was not allowed to sit next to a black man on a bench' – and appalled by the jingoism in Britain during the Falklands conflict. As he said, 'If Thatcher and Galtieri wanted to get at each other they should have put them in a field together. Five years from now people will wonder what it was all about.' It was not the sort of statement that would endear him to the relatives of men who fought in that war, and for a show-business personality it seemed the kind of comment best avoided. But Allen liked to speak his mind on issues of the day and curiously his attitude did not seem to affect his box-office returns.

Yet it was as a funny story-teller that he excelled. In Liverpool, he once told the story of the RAF officer named as co-respondent in a divorce case. The man's name cropped up in another case. Then another ... and another. He was due in court for his sixth case as co-respondent but didn't turn up. The judge, wondering where he was, was informed, 'He's at Buckingham Palace getting the Victoria Cross for heroism from her Majesty the Queen.' To which the judge replied ...

It was at this point, Philip Key recalls, that Allen's memory suddenly failed him. The comedian began to think hard and next moment ad-libbed the counsel for both prosecution and defence. Still the line wouldn't come. Ultimately, he had to admit to the audience, 'I've forgotten the end of this story.' Thereafter, he carried on with the rest of his act as though nothing had happened. Key was to say later, 'The smoothness of the Allen act, which allows such gaffes to be forgotten by audiences, had been developed over his years in show-business.'

On his own admission, the comedian loves his audience, and will do anything to make them laugh. He'll change his act if the audience react with him in certain ways, and he loves looking at them, 'They sit there thinking they're in the dark and I can't see them. But I can. One night I even saw a couple making love. But the audience just laughed. They didn't believe me.'

That night in the Liverpool theatre, the audience did not know whether or not to believe the comedian when he said he could not remember the punchline. 'I think Dave was genuine about it,' says Philip Key. At the interval, members of the audience discussed the unfinished joke and tried to put an ending to it. Before the final curtain Allen said, 'I know I've kept you waiting for it ... Well, the judge adjourned the court, had "God Save the Queen" played, and said, "I hope we're not too late".' Strangely, the audience did not find the joke funny; perhaps it had come too late. Allen was inclined to agree.

Key also covered the Manchester show-business scene for the *Daily Post*, and sometimes tried to explain the differences between the Manchester and Liverpool audiences. He found that Merseysiders were more emotional about theatre and regarded it as an informal event, particularly when they came to watch comedians like Dave Allen or Ken Dodd. Mancunians tended to make it a formal event and some of them went to the theatre to be seen. And the Manchester audiences seemed to be more polite than their Liverpool counterparts. Usually, Allen played for two or three weeks at a time in Manchester and the response there was invariably enthusiastic. That September, he arrived in the city for the start of a three-week season at the Palace Theatre, but news of his marriage break-up had preceded him. After outlining his programme at a press reception, he was asked by a young woman reporter 'Are you getting a divorce, Dave?' Unsmilingly, the comedian looked across the hotel room at the girl and said he would not discuss his marriage. To another question, 'Is your marriage on the rocks?' he shrugged and said it was no business of people to inquire about his marriage.

It was soon plain to the pressmen and women present that the comedian would not be drawn on the subject. 'I never discuss my private life', he said with a stern note of finality and quickly moved on to the next item. A look of disappointment showed in the faces of the media people but before they could enquire further, Allen said, 'I'm negotiating with the BBC for a documentary series which may be screened next year.'

To a few of the gossip-writers present, they would have much preferred to hear the comedian discuss, even briefly, a few of his own problems, especially his marriage break-up. As far as they could recall, they had never been able to draw him out on his private life. As always, they felt frustrated.

Philip Key drove from Liverpool to cover the show at the Manchester Palace Theatre and later told the readers of the *Daily Post* that Allen 'tears into religion with some abandonment. Hopefully, God has a sense of humour. He pokes fun at the illogicalities of Bible stories, imagines a black Pope called Leroy, and generally has fun at the expense of God.' Before the interval, the comedian in a dead-pan style, told the audience, 'If there's a God, I'm in trouble.'

Some of the Palace audience had by now been reduced

to hysterical laughter. After the interval, the comedian talked about sex, bodily functions, private parts, and practically every other taboo subject one cared to mention (or not mention). To Philip Key, Allen did the whole thing with such sincerity and clever wit that you could only admire the man for his sheer nerve, and keep laughing. Key concluded:

> Much of his act would be 'X' certificate stuff in any other hands, but Allen's command of words and his easy-going style seem to make everything he says acceptable. He even manages to get a laugh out of nuclear war pointing out the daftness of the home safety guide published by the Home Office in the event of nuclear attack.

Wherever he went on his tour with *An Evening with Dave Allen*, the comedian resolutely kept his silence about the rumours of a rift in his marriage. Despite the growing number of show-business marriage separations and divorces, people were still curious enough to ask why, particularly if the couple happened to be, as in this case, Dave Allen and Judith Stott. Off-stage, it was hinted that Allen was a complex character, somewhat of a loner, perhaps even a dreamer. His private life remained a mystery, since scarcely a journalist in the land had ever been inside Maple Croft, his home in Berkshire. Unlike some comedians who liked to talk about their pretty wives, Allen held aloof, unemotional about marriage; yet friends in Australia could say that Dave and Judith had been very much in love in those early days in Sydney and that the comedian agonized every time she had to go to England for stage or screen engagements. However, the image he projected in show-business circles was that of a loner. It was not surprising, for most of the time, apart from working on his TV series, he travelled alone which meant he was away from Judith and the children for lengthy periods during the year. Peter Whitmore, producer/director of the *Dave Allen at Large* series, expressed sadness at the news that the comedian's marriage was breaking up. 'I had grown to like Dave a lot during the years we teamed up on the series,' he recalls, 'and I hoped that he and Judith could patch it up. To me, Dave was always a nice man, a considerate person and I was surprised that this should happen to him.'

Almost a year after the first rumours of a rift in their relationship, the Allens were divorced. That February morning in 1983, the comedian arrived at the High Court in London and looked anxious to have the whole matter over as soon as possible. After the hearing, Miss Stott told waiting reporters, 'Everyone gets divorced these days. It's so boring.' Her words seemed to disguise her true feelings. To onlookers, she looked tense and unhappy. Her previous marriage had ended in divorce in 1963.

This bleak winter's morning Allen himself managed to smile. The divorce had been on the grounds that they had lived apart for more than two years. As he walked away from the court he was pressed by reporters for a statement, but predictably he steadfastly refused. To another question, he said, 'I have nothing to say about my divorce.' Next day the *Daily Express* headlined their brief report of the proceedings, 'DIVORCE WITH A SMILE FOR COMEDIAN DAVE ALLEN'. It was the kind of heading that wouldn't endear the comedian to some people less likely to lionize show-business stars. None the less, he remained consistent in his attitude throughout the ten months of the 'rift' reports, ensuring that his children were not drawn into the messy affair.

Judith Stott had turned up at the divorce hearing in black as a 'last laugh' at the comedian. 'The theatre is in my blood and I could not resist it', she said later. The disclosure in court that she and her husband had lived apart for two years came as a surprise to friends who now surmised that the marriage had run into trouble some time before that. She now made no secret of her bitterness, especially as she had given up her acting career to help her husband.

As far as she was concerned, it was a black comedy. To Judith, it had always been 'David', and she could say they had happy days together with their children. Eventually, she claimed, he became detached from herself and the children, 'He seemed to think money was the answer to everything,' she said. 'I don't know what it is about comedians – but they don't seem to be able to face real-life situations.' Being married to a comedian, she reflected, was certainly no laughing matter.

With such a hectic schedule, Allen had scarcely time to dwell on his divorce, though friends were surprised to find his name linked that April with an American woman with whom Judith alleged he had 'set up home' in London's exclusive Knightsbridge. The comedian refused to comment. He was now busy making a comedy series for ITV, having switched from the BBC a few months before. He had signed a £100,000 contract for three specials, but trouble over the show came to a head early on in the shooting.

The comedian had complained about what he said were inadequate props, scenery and special effects. Being an acknowledged perfectionist, he insisted on improvements. Thames described it as only a temporary hitch. By now Allen had not only the reputation of shunning publicity but being occasionally prickly. Someone who worked on the Thames series remarked, 'Dave's a comedian but I can't say there are many laughs involved in working with him.'

The middle 1980s continued to be a time of both laughter and tears for Allen. *An Evening with Dave Allen*, his most important stage show, continued to do well at the box-office, his TV specials were seldom out of the top ratings, and he found time to visit Australia. There was something about Australia that stimulated him. Going there meant not only an increase in his bank balance but seemed essential so that he could distance himself occasionally from the insularity of England. More important still, he found that a warm welcome usually awaited him.

But by late 1985 he was becoming increasingly worried about his brother John and stayed on in England. Despite the treatment he had paid for, his brother's condition had grown worse. He was drinking heavily and was out of work. His last job had been as a stage hand with the Royal

Shakespeare Company; after that, he was homeless. Allen and his brother Peter, who still worked with the *Irish Times* in Dublin, did all they could for their brother, but had to admit the position seemed hopeless. Soon John ended up in a single room in St Mungret's Hostel in Earl's Court, a grim building that houses down-and-outs.

Early in January 1986, John Tynan O'Mahony was found dead there after a fall from his fifth-storey window. Dave and his brother Peter were utterly shaken by the news. They knew they had done everything possible to save their brother, but it was no use; John was too far gone. He was buried in a cold, windswept North London cemetery. Allen himself was there, accompanied by the only other member of the family present, his brother Peter. A small group turned up from Fleet Street, among them Irish-born journalist Tom McGurk who was moved by the solemn scene before him.

Recalling the bleakness of the scene, McGurk says today, 'Dave Allen was in tears. A sad-looking figure in the cold beside the grave, he waved away journalists who wanted a quote from him. "I am not talking about my brother", he whispered. It was an understandable response from someone who had painfully watched the tragedy of his brother unfold before him.'

Later, he told the inquest that his brother John had had an alcoholic problem and became increasingly confused before his death – but he never spoke of killing himself. The Westminster coroner, Dr Paul Knapman, said there was no clear evidence of intention to commit suicide and recorded an open verdict. Cause of death was multiple injuries. The inquest heard that John O'Mahony suffered advanced cirrhosis of the liver and had a rare form of duodenal cancer which would have killed him within two years. Allen said that his brother had been receiving psychiatric treatment, but did not know he had cancer.

To his friends, John Tynan O'Mahony's death came as a shock. Gerry Maxin, who worked with him in Butlin's holiday camps in the 1950s, regarded his death as a tragedy. In his London-based theatrical agency he had hanging on the wall above his desk a picture of Johnny

O'Mahony, as he always called him, beside himself as a Red Coat. 'I understand why Dave Allen is so broken up by his brother's death', Maxin said. 'I think of Johnny as a lovable man, a good comedian, and a friend for life.'

Later, at his home outside Dublin, Peter O'Mahony spoke quietly about his dead brother. He said that Dave and John were particularly close; they were the funny men and he was the straight man. John revelled in Dave's success; he continued to share his happiness and anxieties. Dave understood what his brother was going through in those last agonizing months in London. Peter said that drink eventually destroyed his brother. As he explained to Baz Bamigboye in the *Daily Mail*, 'He would drink a few ales and then down some gin-and-tonics. It ruined his inside and both Dave and I took turns to help him, to encourage him to give it up, to try to make something of his life.'

Peter O'Mahony could become emotional about the death of his brother. As he said,

> My God, Dave tried harder than any of us, and he'd do anything to have his brother with him now. He is cut up at what has happened. But really about five years ago the drink had become an illness with John. Neither Dave nor myself could get him to ease down. Dave had had his own problems in his life, but thank God he has overcome them and he hoped John might overcome his, but it wasn't to be.

Peter was convinced that his brother John could have made the top as a comedian, except that he felt perhaps he wasn't good enough to be a comedian who could do a stand-up act in front of cameras and TV lights, or maybe he lacked confidence in himself. It was a puzzling situation and he admitted that neither he nor Dave ever fully understood.

19   At Home in Kensington

Since his divorce, Allen had been living in a pretty Victorian house in Kensington, with polished wood floors and oriental rugs. French windows led to the small country garden he was creating. His home reflected his bachelor status and his priorities. The living-room was filled with his canvases and paints, his music, his books. To the casual visitor, it was the ideal place to relax, even if Allen didn't always agree.

People were surprised to learn that the comedian painted in his spare time; in fact he insisted in taking time off from his stage and screen work. He needed space and tranquillity to paint, to garden, to read, to stand and stare. Friends found he was able to relax. At fifty, he also enjoyed working alone in the theatre because it meant he could alter his act as he went along, start at the end and work back to the beginning if he felt like it. Even so, he was happy 'darting in and out' of his various professional pursuits as actor, interviewer, documentarian, comic.

He made time to have his children stay with him – they lived also with their mother – and worried about their welfare. Sometimes his daughter Jane dropped into the house at Kensington to cook for him or make tea as he worked on a new canvas. Usually around the house he wore a loose shirt and trousers, and for a man blessed with the Irish gift of the gab, he could paint for hours in silence, or with music playing in the background. The paintings like the house were unexpectedly pretty and included Impressionist landscapes and garden scenes, made up of coloured dots. Occasionally when a friend called he had work in progress on the easel and the rug was strewn all round with half-squeezed tubes of oil paint.

He painted whenever he found the time – at home, on holidays, on tour. He never had an art lesson and said he didn't want to. 'Maybe I'm doing it all wrong,' he'd remark, 'but I love breaking the rules.' The rebel in him had the knack of surfacing in the strangest ways. On a more serious note, he told Lynn Barber of the *Sunday Express*, 'I paint because I want to paint. I love painting, but I wouldn't want to become a painter. And I wouldn't sell the paintings because for me they're a series of little memories or emotions which nobody knows about except me.' Friends believed that any art gallery would be happy to hang his paintings.

As he grew older, he tended to become more suspicious of journalists and their intentions. For instance, when Miss Barber first sought an interview the comedian's agent stipulated beforehand that she could ask about anything 'except, you *know*, personal things – his divorce, or money'. He was prepared to talk about his work only. Naturally, she felt curtailed, but nevertheless decided to go ahead with the interview, as Allen's comic world fascinated her. Unsurprisingly, she received some predictable answers, nothing really new. Allen retailed a few funny stories and although they were amusing in the telling, later in print they looked prosaic.

She admitted she found him a gifted raconteur, an Irishman of considerable charm with a magic carpet of words. Nor was he reluctant to talk about his recently deceased brother John Tynan O'Mahony. In a low voice he recalled, 'I was aware that he had a severe alcohol problem for some years. He had been to various agencies to get help. I used to drive him every day from the hostel to Westminster Hospital for psychiatric treatment.' At this point of the interview he was frank and talkative, however his mood changed when Miss Barber brought up the question of money and his divorce. It was obvious she had broken the rules and the comedian didn't like it.

When she reminded him that his former wife, Judith Stott, had said that he regarded money as the answer to everything, and that being married to a comedian was no laughing matter, Allen told her bluntly, 'I prefer not to be associated with any of this.' Miss Barber persisted, 'You do admit that money is the answer to everything?'

'Not particularly so. No.' By now the smile had vanished from his face and he looked uneasy.

The interview was suddenly at an end. He rose and proceeded to show her politely to the door on the pretext that he had an urgent appointment somewhere else. Lynn Barber knew she had trespassed into private territory and was being thrown out like the intruder she was. She summed up for her paper, 'Mr Allen remains a very private – and likeable man.'

Life in Kensington was not altogether a bed of roses for the mercurial comedian. Drivers blasting their horns were likely to find themselves taken to task by a frustrated Allen who told them he lived there and did not want his life subjected to horn-blowers. He could never see the need for horns in cars, other than to release frustration. At this time, unnecessary horn-blowing was one of the many *bêtes noires* which inhabited his life. He conducted a one-man battle against irritations and aggravations of the hi-tech profit-orientated, uniform world around him, refusing to condone any of it. And whether he was filling in immigration forms, or struggling to open the plastic bags supplied in a roll by supermarkets, his rebellion was absolute.

He was, of course, fortunate in having the wit to utilize his prejudices and pet hates to entertain audiences. His philosophy about humour hadn't changed. He accepted that humour was not so much about laughing at other people as at what you did yourself and how you reacted. He was aware, too, that he was no longer in the first flush of youth. Talking about his life at home, he told a *Times* reporter, 'I'm quite laid back. The days go very quickly. I sit down to write something and get up to make a cup of tea and it's seven o'clock in the evening. I suppose that's one way of knowing you're getting older.'

Undoubtedly he had become more thoughtful, more introspective, as was reflected in his humour and conversation. He was conscious more than ever before of what he called the loss of individuality in society. As he said,

> If I think of the names of the past – Franco, Hitler, Chamberlain, Churchill, Roosevelt ... whatever they were, they were individuals. Now there's a great grey quality about everyone. Even in my own business there used to be agents who were characters. Now there are lawyers. Thirty years ago I would shake hands for a contract. Now there's clause upon clause and it just goes on and becomes greyer. People have got their heads down now.

Despite his divorce, he remained close to his children. By now his son Edward, aged nineteen, was a member of the National Youth Theatre. The year before, 1985, the boy had been expelled from Radley College after he was discovered smoking marijuana in the grounds of the £4,935-a-year Oxfordshire public school, and he now found himself in trouble again. In the company of Jimmy Tarbuck, junior, young Allen had been stopped by police as they drove through Chelsea at midnight. Both youths and another youngster in the car were taken to Chelsea police station and quizzed for several hours. The police claimed they had cannabis on them. They were given bail after being warned that they could face drug charges.

Informed of the incident, Allen himself commented, 'I am aware of what has happened. My interests are obviously to protect my son.' Later, the police decided not to press charges against the three youths. It was said that the comedian was upset by the glare of publicity the story attracted and decided to make no further comment about the matter. It was a time when the children of some other showbiz business stars, including Richard Harris's son Jamie, were in trouble over the possession of drugs and the public did not really regard it any longer as sensational news. All Jimmy Tarbuck would say was, 'There is no trouble with my son.' Relieved that the incident was over, Allen commented, 'I don't think the incident is good, but then again I don't think it's bad.'

*

By now he was looking forward to another visit to Australia. There was nothing he enjoyed more and the prospect of renewing old friendships and making new friends tended to raise his spirits enormously. Although his hair was greyer and the French cigarettes were missing, Australians nevertheless found that his wit had by no means dimmed; he was as sharp as ever – and as gentle – as ever. And it was to this apparent paradox that the veteran comedian attributed his success and durability.

That October 1986, as he rushed, tousle-haired and almost furtive, through the crowded foyer of his Sydney hotel, somebody shouted from the reception desk, 'Mr Allen, sir. We have a dozen telephone messages for you.' Glancing quickly towards the desk, he said, 'Ah! It doesn't surprise me. That'll be the Church of Rome, the anti-corruption squad, the liquor and gaming boys and probably my agent!' He was back in the city after four years, and it seemed that everybody wanted to greet him at once. He refused to take the hotel lift, explaining at the same time to an eager young journalist, 'Lifts are weird'.

After a pause, he said with an air of mystery, 'What is it about lifts that makes two people who are deep in conversation stop as they get in a lift and stand silently and watch one, two, three light up in red numbers?' As he answered his own question, he pulled a funny face, and decided that everyone was thinking at that moment about the lift falling. 'I am', he said solemnly. It wasn't that he had a phobia about lifts. Lifts had a phobia about him. Twice he had been caught in one, and prayed to the God he harried so relentlessly, that deliverance would arrive.

Funnily, he found some things weird that other people regarded as normal. Telephones, for instance. 'We have telephones to communicate and then we have a machine to answer the machine. Or another machine plays you musak. I don't like musak generally and if they play you a piece of music that's quite nice they come in and interrupt the music.' Similarly, underground railways and aeroplanes got to him. The underground, along with lifts, was another place in his view where people lost their sense of humour. He found that no-one in the underground talked to anyone – they read papers or books. He wasn't unduly surprised. As he reasoned, 'When you think hard about it, it is an unnatural state to be going at one hundred kilometres an hour – underground!'

He saw jets as 'a big flying sneeze'. Everything everybody did on board got recycled. Where did all that sweat and flaking skin go? What he really wanted to know was how much heavier were jets after a long flight. It was the comedian once more seeing life as a bizarre comedy. He admitted he concentrated on these things to take his mind off the 'hosties' who started terrifying everybody with their useless safety drill. When he indulged in such flights of fancy, his mind seemed to wander all over the place, like a Joycean stream of consciousness. For instance, Cleopatra at that time was one of his favourite stock characters. He saw her as the first feminist. 'I can see her pinching Mark Antony in the face and saying, 'It's my turn now. I'm entitled to an orgasm!' He liked to say that it was the Cleopatras who were responsible for the falling birthrate. 'It's got to the stage where it's the *men* who are faking the orgasm.'

Journalists in Australia had always found the comedian a rich source for copy. As long as they avoided his private life they could expect his co-operation. Joanna Parsons of *Woman's Day* interviewed him early in the morning in his hotel bedroom. His eyes were bloodshot, he yawned and stretched his arms above his head, and wondered what lay before him. The conversation went as follows:

Parsons: Good morning, Mr Allen. Your office arranged an interview for me to ask you twenty random questions. It's supposed to reveal your inner personality.

Allen (weakly): They did? … They didn't tell me … I was talking until 5 a.m. about President Kennedy.

Parsons: What are your likes and dislikes?

Allen: I'll have a cup of tea and think about that one …

Parsons: How much right do you think fans have to details of a TV star's life?

Allen: You know what happened to me once: some journalist came in here, sat down and opened up with, 'Now tell me about your love life.' [Excitedly ruffling his hair] I mean, fancy anyone being fool enough to ask a question like that!

[Miss Parsons hurriedly scratches out something in her notebook.]

Allen: You know, the other morning I woke up to find five teenage girls standing around my bed, giggling down at me. Heaven knows how they managed to get in.

Parsons: What did you do?

Allen [smilingly]: What else could I do: I was trapped. We talked for an hour and a half.

Parsons: Have you thought about your taste in women?

Allen: Yeah, but whatever I say, I'm going to offend somebody ... is there any tea in that pot ...? [Picks up the phone] Could we have another tray of tea, please dear?

Parsons: How much does criticism worry you? For instance, one critic recently called you a 'professional Irishman' –

Allen [sitting bolt upright]: Who said that? That's a very stupid remark, I'm proud of being Irish. I'm very nationalistic, but people always tend to be more nationalistic away from home [broods over tea].

Parsons: Are you superstitious like most Irishmen?

Allen [with beautiful vagueness]: I do have theatrical superstitions, like whistling in the dressing-room being bad luck. One time a Scottish piper came into my dressing-room, whistling his head off. I told him to go outside, turn round and spit – that's to break the bad luck. I had the devil's job trying to convince him I meant it. We nearly came to blows.

Parsons: Are you happiest in a crowd or when alone?

Allen: I'm not a Garbo nut or anything like that. I love talking.

Parsons: And women?

Allen: Hell, I don't know. You may have hated redheads all your life. Then one day a redhead comes along ... and you love redheads. If you go around trying to define people you could end up in a psycho ward. Now put the notebook away, girl, and let's just talk. [Picks up the phone] Do you think I could have another tray of tea please, dear ...

An Evening with Dave Allen filled theatres across Australia. For the first time, the comedian toured the small towns as well as the big cities and was surprised, as he said, not to come across a Mary Whitehouse or two in his travels. 'They are everywhere,' he laughed. 'Whether in the UK, America or Australia there are people who object to some of my material.' He found, however, that some Irish people did not like his jokes about the confessional box nor Roman Catholicism. Undeterred, he moved on from place to place, like a travelling salesman selling humour instead of food commodities.

By now his house in Kensington seemed a million miles away. It was proving one of the most enjoyable tours of his career, convincing him yet again that humour was universal, that people everywhere identified with painful hangovers, eccentric bishops and Popes of Rome. Audiences discovered that there was an underlying seriousness to all his jokes. People found that the philosopher in him was never far from the surface. As time passed, he was becoming less of a joker. Friends wondered if he was perhaps too analytical for his own good, but it was the secret of his humour, a product of his observation and his vivid imagination. It was this approach that made him different from most other comics.

20   The Bishop's Waltz

The successful Australian tour behind him, Allen accepted an unusual invitation in early March 1987. It had come from a *real* bishop and this made a change after his comic impersonations of popes, vicars and bishops, and as 'God's Own Comedian' the irony was not lost on him.

At that time, Irish television (RTE) was presenting *Saturday View*, a weekly chat show with the different presenters asked to invite their own guests. Walton Empey, the Church of Ireland Bishop of Meath and Kildare, decided it would be interesting to invite Dave Allen, his favourite comedian, and was delighted that he accepted.

To the majority of Irish people, it was a curious choice for the bishop to make, for Allen had the reputation for lampooning clergy and telling *risqué* stories, so they wondered how the amiable Empey was going to handle the rebellious comedian. They reckoned without his innate sense of humour. The bishop, a burly figure, had a glorious laugh and was said to enjoy Allen's off-beat wit and black comedy. He was a man of the world, had served in the British army and later became a clergyman and administered in the bleak territories of New Brunswick to a parish which had not had a resident curate for twenty-eight years.

For relaxation, he now walked and fly-fished and was popular with the people of his diocese. There was a well-embellished story about the catching of his last salmon in the west of Ireland, a story Allen would surely enjoy, if not tell himself on stage. Empey hooked the salmon, dropping the fly across a slimy bed of weeds and rubbish. The salmon ran across the pool and returned three times. He could not figure out how to land it. But he was determined not to let the salmon go free. Maddened, he waded in after it, sinking in the slime and his clothes were covered as far as his armpits. He managed to get the salmon and slooshed back to the shore, 'thanking the Lord that no one had seen the performance.' He was sitting on the bank, emptying out the weedy water, when behind him trilled a clear soprano voice. 'Oh, Bishop, what a fine fish!' A local nun had witnessed the whole thing.

Bishop Empey wasn't afraid to retail the story to friends after a day's pheasant or duck-shooting; indeed, some of them reckoned he might even make 'a respectable comic' himself, so assured was he at telling funny stories. For days he worked on the questions for *Saturday View*, hardly giving a thought to the likelihood that Allen might monopolize the show. The comedian himself flew into Dublin that March morning determined to attend the rugby international at Lansdowne Road between Ireland and Wales. Luckily for him an RTE executive gave him his stand ticket and in the early afternoon he walked, almost unrecognized, to the ground. As a boy, he had attended games there and the big match atmosphere came back to him again. 'Wonderful', he remarked to an old Dublin pal later.

He was that night accorded a theatrical entry to *Saturday View*, the orchestra playing in the studio and a voice exclaiming, 'It's Dave Allen!' He smiled as he took his seat beside presenter Bishop Empey and the special panel of four. When asked why Irish entertainers had gone right to the top of the British entertainment ladder, and if they really had a unique talent in this sphere, Allen thought they had. As an example, he said Eamonn Andrews had gone to England in the fifties and become the envy of every boxing commentator. Entertainers like Val Doonican left Ireland because of the restrictive size of the country and the lack of opportunity. When he himself decided to leave for London, he worked in strip clubs, to the disgust of his mother, and in working-men's clubs all over the place.

Empey: We are really quite superior, aren't we? [laughter] Tell me, Dave, do you miss Dublin?

Allen: I don't broadcast it, but I come back quite a lot. I come into Ireland and wander about. Last year I spent eight full days wandering about the West of Ireland. It's lovely, it's beautiful, it's great.

Empey: I think of comedians as blokes who get up and tell gags and one-liners. I haven't heard you do that, you seem to take situations and tease them out. I mean, does the term *comedian* really suit you?

Allen: Yeah. I really am what I am. I am a talker and hopefully will get laughs and make people listen and probably sometimes score a point. When I started, I used to do a Jerry Lewis impersonation, that's what I was, because I felt I had to hide behind somebody; you always hide behind somebody, whoever it might be; and then I started to tell jokes in working-men's clubs and, between telling jokes, if I was sitting with somebody, I'd be talking about my childhood or my life. People would look at me and say, 'Dave, why don't you talk about that on stage? It's much more interesting and enjoyable than the jokes.' I remember one thing I said was that I really disliked adults; to me, they were real dickheads, they really were. Adults used to say things to me like, 'How long since I've seen you?' and I'd reply, 'Five years.' And they'd say, 'You have grown.' My mother actually said to me one day when I was up a tree, 'Don't climb the tree.' I said 'I am up there', but she said, 'If you fall out of it don't come running to me.' I used to ask myself what is she talking about, so I vowed when I grew up I'd never be an adult, I wouldn't grow old. Eventually though, I got married and had children. One day I was in my house and looking at my eldest son in the garden with my younger son and there is some sort of confrontation going on.

As he uses funny voice sounds to indicate thuds and blows the audience laugh, and they laugh again as he describes how he ran down the garden and threw blows at his eldest son who has knocked down his small brother.

Raising his voice he says, 'I am beating hell out of the bigger fellow, shouting at him at the same time, "How dare you … You'll learn one thing from me in life, that you do not walk around hitting people who are smaller than you." As I beat the hell out of him, I am aware I've become an adult, the very thing I abhorred as a child.'

Before presenter Empey can come in, Allen continues at a furious pace, 'As a child I hated cabbage. I really did. But my parents would say, "Eat it." I'd look at them and say, "I don't like it." My mother would insist, "Yes, you do, Dave. Go on, eat it." She would go on and on. However, if there was an adult in the house my mother would never get up and say, "What's this on the plate here?"

' "It's cabbage."

' "Eat it!" '

The studio rocks with laughter and Bishop Empey has almost given up trying to get in a word of his own. Fascinated by Allen's way of telling a story, he listens as the comedian continues, 'Think of the starving children of the world', my mother would say. I used to answer her back, "Put it in the bloody envelope and send it to them." Anyway, they'd probably send it back with the message, "We don't like cabbage either".'

He is monopolizing the show, yet no-one dares to stop him. For the studio audience, it is proving hugely enjoyable. He goes on, 'I mean there are things in my memory of childhood … For instance, the restrictions on coming home in time … and that terrible thing of being a boy of fourteen and your parents warning you, "Don't be late!" A boy whispers beside you, "What time is it?" You reply, also in a whisper, "A quarter to eleven." You look at him and utter, "Oh, God." You're a wreck. You're running towards the house, breathless muttering to yourself, "Please don't hit me …" You have arrived at the house and it is in darkness and they've gone to bed, and you open the door, but the door creaks; soon all the floorboards seem to be creaking, they've become Judases.'

By now the audience cannot refrain from laughing and Bishop Empey is also laughing his head off. Unruffled, Allen continues, scarcely taking notice of anyone around him; 'As I've said, the house is in darkness and they've gone to bed and I'm inside, making my way on tiptoe down the corridor, when suddenly the lights are on and my parents are sitting there, Mummy and Daddy ... Himmler and Goering ... and they come at you, with my father exclaiming, "I told you ... nine o'clock ... I told you ... things can happen to you outside". All the time he's beating the crab out of me in the corridor?'

Empey: I hope my family is listening to this and taking special notice. Dave, you said to me earlier about stress having an influence on the sort of thing you do ...

By now, Allen has calmed down and looks relaxed. Although his emotional imput into his story-telling has obviously been considerable, he looks in Empey's direction and says he has read somewhere that every two illnesses out of three are related to stress. Amid silence, he continues, 'We're under pressures. I started to read up about stress. Stress basically is what your body creates. For example, it's energy, a mixture of your brain creating with chemicals energy for your body either to run from or fight whatever it is that is causing you anxiety. It goes back to early man where a caveman would come around and see a tiger and he would immediately go into stress. Great oceans of energy would suddenly be in your system. You'd either run away or pick up a rock and brain the bastard.[laughter]

Empey: My mother-in-law is down there ...

Allen: Is she one of *those*, too? [more laughter] You see in our society you can find that somebody puts you under stress. Your boss might say, 'Is it possible to have a word with you?' When the boss says that your body is immediately in stress, instead of picking up a chair and braining the bastard, you sit there and you get into more and more stress. You see people with cars who are subjected to the most extraordinary stress. You get behind a row of cars and blow a horn, the heads turn in unison, like hens. I go through it myself. I hear a horn and I instantly think he is blowing it at me. I mean, it can be two miles away. There are people who have the ability ... have you ever been at traffic lights? ... red ... and the fellow behind you goes beeb and it goes green ... and you swear, 'You swine, how can you do that ...?'

As the audience laughs, he pauses for a moment and sips from a glass of water. As the laughter recedes, he goes on, 'I live in Kensington and as soon as I get behind the wheel of a car – and I'm sure everyone is the same – I say no man is a man any more, no man is a chap or a fellow ... he's a bastard – they are all bastards – hairy bastard, fat bastard, small bastard ... that's the way I think. If I'm walking up the street I'm not worried about space. I don't want to take over people when I'm on a pavement. I don't try cutting up people. But when I get behind a car I'm possessive, I'll run the bastard down if he gets between me and another car. I'll run into him. It's this anger.' [more laughter]

Amid laughter he continues the story about red and green lights, impatient drivers and comes to the conclusion that a certain driver is a lunatic, so he decides to play this fellow like a gentle soul. 'I get out of the car and as I walk back to him he starts to wind the window up and I grab it, and I say, "Are you alright ... I mean, are you having a heart attack ... do you want the kiss of life?" The man at the wheel rants away at me incomprehensibly. I try to explain to him that a little old lady has stepped in front of my car and I stopped, that if I'd been in a hurry I'd have run her over but I didn't. And I hear myself saying to the man, 'If I had a head like yours, I'd have it circumcized.'

It is the best one-liner in the show and the audience responds with prolonged applause. Bishop Empey interjects, 'I know exactly what Dave is talking about. I thought I was one of the oddities of the world. I'm glad to see someone else admitting this.'

Allen [calmly]: We are all the same.

He goes on to talk about more traffic jams and seems to be prolonging the joke unduly, although the audience do not think so. One of the panel obviously feels that enough is enough of traffic jams and, looking across in his direction, says, 'Here you are surrounded by one of the pillars of the church and most viewers know that Dave Allen sometimes dresses up like a bishop, sometimes even as the Pope ...

Allen: I'm promoting myself.

Panellist: What is there about clerics that either turns you on or off?

Allen [thoughtfully]: I think it's making a face at authority. I mean, I go back to my childhood, I was educated by the clergy ... the Gestapo ... The clergy themselves have great humour, there's no doubt about that; it's the interpretation of what people get that's puzzling. I was doing a sketch in a graveyard – I like graveyards, they are good places for laughs – the idea being about the man who invented down payment on hire purchase coffins. This man hadn't finished paying before he died so he only got half a coffin. So we are walking up the road towards the graveyard and we are all in black, beautifully dressed and we have mourners – we're an authentic kosher funeral – and coming down towards us is another funeral – a *real* funeral – and we have this coffin with a pair of legs sticking out the back and we both divide and we split, and the faces on these people – these legs are actually wobbling; now the vicar of their lot comes up to me afterwards and he is the personification of an English curate: he has the most enormous Adam's apple and the collar is about five sizes too big, dandruff like snow storms, and he says in a funny voice, 'I do enjoy your shows very much, but you do tend – how can I put it? – to portray us clergymen as stupid assholes,' [laughter]

Panellist: What is the reaction of the laity by and large to your shows?

Allen: Let me tell you, first, of one of the loveliest sketches I ever did. It was about the death of an old actor. Imagine the scene: he is being cremated and there is the coffin and the small curtain area behind it and the old clergyman pays tribute to this knight of the theatre who has brought the Bard to the stage, providing pleasure and enjoyment, and he is rambling on ... then he says, 'In terms of the theatrical profession he is about to take his last final call.' With that, the curtains open and the coffin disappears behind the aperture and the curtains close. And the congregation start to applaud. Suddenly the curtains open and the coffin comes out and takes a call.

It is noticeable that the volume of applause for the comedian's black humour is not nearly as great as for his stories about traffic jams and infuriated drivers. Presumably, for an enjoyable night out, some of the audience prefer to forget funerals and coffins. When he is asked again if he gets nasty letters about his TV shows, the comedian admits that he does. He recalls the story about an old bishop and his crozier and the various nuns who come up and kiss the bishop's ring and go away. Then a rather beautiful young virginal, clean-faced girl kisses the ring and the crozier becomes erect. Later Allen is standing at the bar counter and a little man comes over to him and remarks, 'That's it, I've had it with you. No more!' He says portraying the Pope like that and giving the impression of an erection is too much. I tell him that it is not the Pope and that, 'If you look at the costume the actor is wearing that it's the Archbishop of Canterbury.' The little man looks at me and says, "Oh, *that's* alright".' [laughter]

One or two elderly ladies in the audience look embarrassed and refrain from joining in the laughter; a few others laugh politely. The majority however rock with laughter. Bishop Empey smiles and says nothing. Someone in the audience – an old soldier – asks if Allen has any funny stories about soldiers and is told, 'There are too many of you.' At this point the conversation switches to the Irish UN force abroad and their peace-keeping mission. At the mention of the word *peace*, Allen remarks in a serious tone, 'The word peace, that's important.'

Bishop Empey thanks the 'irreverent' Dave Allen for accepting his invitation to come on the show. Bill Whelan has composed *The Bishop's Waltz* for the show, as a tribute to Empey and now proceeds to conduct the studio orchestra in the catchy piece of music. Whelan, years before, had written the music for *Bloomfield*, the movie starring Richard Harris. After the chat show, he joined Allen and the panellists in the hospitality room.

'I was meeting Dave Allen for the first time,' he recalls, 'and he came across to me as most personable. He didn't act the star but mixed easily among us all. As we talked, he recalled the match that afternoon at Lansdowne Road, also Bishop Empey's handling of the show. I agreed with him that the bishop made a friendly presenter.' To Whelan, Allen was simply a very funny man as well as an ordinary bloke who fitted easily into company.

21 Laughs in Belfast

Undeterred by talk of bombs, bullets, Prods and Taigs, Allen flew into Belfast that October 1988 determined to make the people laugh. At the airport, instead of taking a taxi, he boarded a bus for the twenty-mile round journey to the Europa Hotel and proceeded to chat up the other passengers, as though eager to get the 'feel' of the place.

He had expressed no apprehension about coming when Michael Barnes, director of the Belfast Arts Festival, extended the invitation, and already it looked as if his performances at the Grand Opera House would be a sell-out. Sadly, Belfast had experienced some of the worst violence in Northern Ireland since 1969 – even the Grand Opera House hadn't escaped the bombs – but life and laughter continued as people showed their remarkable resilience. Belfast had a tradition for comedy, going back to the old Empire Theatre where Dublin comic Jimmy O'Dea was among those popular with audiences. Later, the city's own Frank Carson carved a special niche for himself before he sought fame and riches in Blackpool and elsewhere.

Eddie McIlwaine of the *Belfast Telegraph* is a close observer of the variety and theatre scene and says without hesitation, 'Belfast people love to laugh at religious jokes.' He saw it as one of the reasons for Dave Allen's popularity. Neither the Protestants nor the Catholics got upset when he poked fun at them, although most of the time he leaned more on the Catholics. McIlwaine felt Belfast theatre-goers were inclined to give priority to light entertainment. 'What I mean is they will book for a Frank Carson or a Dave Allen show before a play by Pirandello or Pinter, and I think this has been the case for a long time. Comedy attracts people from both sides of the divide and has become increasingly popular, partly due I'd imagine to the troubles when people sought light relief.' McIlwaine drew a distinction between Carson and Allen. 'Carson, with his Belfast background and idiomatic humour, has always been a big attraction, and his one-liners never fail to raise a laugh; Allen, on the other hand, is seen as more sophisticated and subtle and some of his story-telling can be hilarious. No one here has ever objected to his jokes and both Protestants and Catholics enjoy him, even if a few people do regard him as "a dirty comic".'

Back in 1980 Allen had first wanted to visit the city, but engagements in Australia ruled that out. But he solemnly pledged he would one day play the Grand Opera House, and in 1984 he kept that promise. On arrival in Belfast, he said, 'There were times when I thought I'd never make it. One consolation is the jokes I'd have told in 1980 are stale now. I've a whole bagful of new ones, bang up to date ...'

It was the first time that Eddie McIlwaine met the comedian and was impressed by his unforced conversation and cheerfulness. Since Belfast people loved earthy comics, he had no doubt that Allen would appeal greatly to them. At that time, the comedian was said to have made a career out of poking fun at religion and getting away with it. 'We are delighted Dave is coming to town even four years late', remarked theatre executive Robert Agnew. 'He is one of the few entertainers capable of handling a one-man show on such a big stage as the Opera House.'

Belfast audiences wondered if Allen would do his famous impersonation of Ian Paisley – the one television audiences found so funny – but he omitted it – some said wisely – at the Opera House. It wasn't exactly the time – nor the place – for lampooning Dr Paisley. Nevertheless, the comedian rocked the house with laughter, as Jane Bell of the *Belfast Telegraph* told her readers. As she wrote,

He served up more than two-and-a-half hours of scorching satire and biting wit, with 'no holds barred' jokes about religion, sex and human stress. Unflinchingly, the comedian laid bare society's taboos and follies and he sent up everybody mercilessly and they loved it. On the stage he looked a solitary figure with only his trademark props – a stool and a glass but he managed to paint a full spectrum of characters who illuminated his tales – from a born again Nazi park-keeper to a turncoat duck called Judas.

Miss Bell concluded:

Unshackled from the propriety of Auntie BBC *An Evening with Dave Allen* is liberally laced with four-letter words, but it is unlikely to ruffle the sensibilities of those who really enjoy his brand of humour. And there is an intimacy between performer and audience that one would not expect in such an imposing theatre. A great many of the fullhouse audience were clearly Dave Allen devotees. Some of the material seemed familiar from his television shows of the seventies, but nobody seemed to mind. They say laughter is the best medicine and last night showed Dave Allen has a patient.

Four years later, in 1988, Michael Barnes had to bring little persuasion on Allen to get him to come back to Belfast. To the festival director, he was a delightful man and a brilliant comedian. He first saw him some years before at the Haymarket in London, luckily managing to get a return ticket at the box-office. That evening, he found himself sitting beside a group of Dutch people who 'laughed their heads off'. So too, was Barnes himself. Fascinated by the comedian's approach, he began to examine why he made people laugh like that. For example, when he joked about the Pope or a bishop he reckoned that Allen was in no way feeling superior to either of them, rather was he saying they were flawed, as he himself was flawed, and others in the human race.

Later, when he saw the comedian at the Theatre Festival in Dublin, he decided he wanted him for the Belfast Festival. Off-stage, he found him a very serious man who was concerned about the problems of the world. In his view, he was more a comic entertainer than a comedian. He had no trepidation about inviting him to Belfast, for the people appreciated the kind of smooth and satirical humour that was Allen's hall mark, and although he used the four-letter word it wasn't in an offensive way and the audiences recognized this.

To Barnes, the impact the comedian was able to make without pulling funny faces, wearing exotic costumes, or doing a knock-about act was extraordinary. The truth was he hardly moved at all on stage, depending more on a grin or a raised eyebrow or a different accent to maximize his punchlines. Allen, he knew, was helped by people's attitude to humour generally. When an audience at the Opera House really wanted to laugh it was capable of lifting the rafters. When the comedian told his religious jokes, he told them with an open mind and audiences did not feel offended; in fact, some of the comedian's best humour was inspired by the Bible, particularly his wonderful story of Noah and the flood.

Something else impressed the festival director. He had brought the comedian to Belfast in Edna O'Brien's play *A Pagan Place* when he gave such a good performance that Barnes decided he could make a living from straight acting. 'I am positive he could', he says today. 'His concentration is superb, his voice is clear and very expressive. I am hoping to present him one day in another serious play. Dave is such an intelligent man and versatile actor.'

Once more, the Opera House was filled for *An Evening with Dave Allen* and as usual he strode on stage using no props, no scenery and no gimmicks, and for nearly three hours kept his audience enthralled. He showed a healthy contempt for politicians – 'They are the only people who can speak with great authority on subjects about which they know nothing.' Like Ken Dodd, he had a habit of exploring old age, and here he emphasized the tell-tale signs – 'the memory fades, the eyes grow long-sighted, hair sprouts in the ears and nose, and skin loses its elasticity – unless you splash out on a facelift, like Nancy Reagan who looks like a bushbaby on a hanger.'

Reviewing for the *Belfast Telegraph*, Grania McFadden summed up:

This is a show of meticulously researched material. Using language that would certainly shock a nun, Allen scrutinizes the soothing vocabulary used by airlines, revealing the 'near misses' and 'emergency landings' as 'hits' and 'crashes'. He also takes some well-aimed swipes at the establishment, and of course religion.

To the delight of the audience, he ended his show with a revealing sketch about teaching a small child how to tell the time. As ever, he sent the audience away with the familiar phrase, 'May your God go with you'. Charles Fitzgerald, critic of the Belfast *News Letter* said that Belfast audiences liked smooth and sophisticated comedians and it was the main reason why they responded so rapturously to Dave Allen. In his view, Belfast had always been a happy hunting-ground for comics, and this had not changed in spite of the troubles. Eddie McIlwaine felt that Belfast was more liberal-minded than Dublin. 'Billy Connolly has done well here in the same way as Dave Allen. Belfast can laugh at itself – and I mean both Protestants, Catholics and everyone else. If a comedian is really funny, they don't mind if he is a Jew or a Muslim, as long as he makes them laugh.'

To McIlwaine, Allen was a comic of the people. He spoke to them in an earthy language and in the theatre they giggled at his sexual innuendoes and ribald humour. 'I think some people found his naughty approach irresistible', McIlwaine said. Off-stage, the comedian drank in pubs near the Grand Opera House, chatted quietly to journalists or to Belfast actors, and was always on the lookout for amusing stories. McIlwaine felt that Allen loved to talk and he had rarely any trouble getting listeners.

Charles Fitzgerald thought that Belfast simply looked up to popular TV comics. 'I think they liked to see them in the flesh and were disappointed if their stage act fell short of expectations.' He had made a study of Dave Allen's brand of comedy. As he watched him on stage, he felt he was not nearly as funny as his screen image, mainly because TV editors could ensure that Allen's sketches, stories and punchlines were razor sharp.

While he agreed that he was a great story-teller with a style of his own, his stage act sometimes overran and when it did it became tiresome. Because Belfast adored comedians it didn't seem to matter however and any star comic was nearly always assured of a full house on a Sunday night.

It was said that Allen was intrigued by the religious question in Belfast and before he left the city had accumulated a dozen funny stories about clergymen and their idiosyncrasies. He found them a warm people and not afraid to laugh at themselves. Frank Carson had always asserted that despite its puritanical image Belfast welcomed comedians. Others argued that Belfast theatre-goers liked blue comedians, or humour with 'a strong tinge of blue'.

An Evening with Dave Allen was travelling well and the comedian had no complaints about box-office receipts. In Liverpool, he met Philip Key, show-business editor of the *Post* and they found much to talk about. To the amiable Key, it hardly seemed six years since the comedian had visited the city, or indeed the north-west. Ironically, he had come to Liverpool to promote his forthcoming appearance in Manchester, where he was due to open at the Palace Theatre for a week. 'It's a simple matter of theatre availability,' Allen said, 'there's no suitable theatre for me in Liverpool.'

Instead, he spent hours looking over the city. He was fascinated by the Albert Dock, he stared at old pictures on the walls at Granada TV, and generally was impressed by the city's progress. That evening, as they dined together in a city hotel, Philip Key found that Allen hadn't changed. Age had not mellowed him and he said he felt, as always, anger and frustration. He complained that life had become too noisy and that wasn't a healthy thing. Despite his greying hairs and new maturity, he assured Key that he wasn't retiring, and hoped to bring the show to America and Canada in the months ahead.

'So you are still proud of your name in lights?' said Key.

Allen smiled.

'No, it means nothing. It doesn't give me any thrill to see my name in big words outside the theatre. It never has – my main concern is to just do the job for which I am being paid.' Key was puzzled about something else. 'What are you calling your show – I mean Michael Jackson calls his the *Bad Tour*, while Barry Humphries has titled his *Back with a Vengeance*?'

Allen was genuinely surprised by the question. 'It's just *An Evening with Dave Allen*. What else should I call it? If you call something a one-man show and then you have other people on, it's just not fair. And it's still unscripted. I change it each night. Only about fifty per cent remains from one night to the next.'

To the experienced Key, the comedian remained one of Britain's top comedians and it was a shame that Liverpool was not seeing the show. He knew better than to ask him personal questions and kept the conversation to show-business. He would be reviewing the show at the Palace Theatre. An Allen evening was an event in itself, different from anything else in the theatre.

A week later, Mancunians packed the Palace for *An Evening with Dave Allen*, and Philip Key wrote in the *Post*, 'Manchester's gain is Liverpool's loss'. The comedian was also in the headlines for another reason. He got up people's noses when he went on the Michael Aspel chat show. Viewers phoned up to complain that his jokes were about people making strange smells.

By now Australian politician Bob Hawke was calling Allen an honorary Australian and it was an apt label. After a tour of England with *An Evening with Dave Allen*, he set out once more in 1989 on a tour down under. He travelled alone as he had done twenty-five years before when he decided to try his luck in that distant land. In Sydney, he denied he was a millionaire, although he said he was 'comfortable'. He looked a trifle wistful as he considered the money on offer at this time for 'irreverence towards religion'. And he suggested the ideal hiding-place for Salman Rushdie, 'The safest place for him would be as a conductor on a London bus, among the great number of

Indians and Pakistanis. But the outriders on police protection would give away the bus, which would be full of MI 5 security men so no one could get on anyway.'

To Australians, the comedian appeared the same, except for his shock of grey hair, his tendency towards overweight, the spectacles he wore, and the missing cigarettes – and he had eased up a little on alcohol. They considered he had made a lucrative living from poking fun at the Christian faiths and would remain in their eyes 'God's Own Comedian'. However, he was taking this opportunity to poke fun at non-Christians and had a word or two to say about Ayatollah Khomeini and his paranoia about Salman Rushdie and *The Satanic Verses*. Trying to be serious for a moment, the comedian said, 'I feel sorry for Mr Rushdie. He hasn't held (Islam) up to ridicule, he's said something about it in a serious novel. If you think about it, the words "publish and be damned" stand up to Rushdie. He's published, and he's been damned.'

Off-stage, he could be caustic. He found in that March of 1989 that Sydney's beaches were a disgrace. As he said, 'I used to go to the beach out here but I don't think they are safe now. Going to the beach now is almost as dangerous as writing a book!' In case people took him too seriously, he would say in the next sentence, 'I am here to make people laugh.' Wherever he went, he had something to say. In Canberra, he talked about comedy. 'Comedy is knowing how vulnerable you are; how silly and how trite and how petty and how wonderful and all those things that make a human being.'

He said it was very easy to fall into the trap of gathering ethnic gags and throwing your barbs of humour at other people, whether they were black or Greek or Italian or Jewish or any of the stereotypes. That to him was not humour, it had got nothing to do with humour. Although he said put-down Irish jokes were not his cup of tea, he proceeded to tell what he said was the only Irish joke he really liked: 'The foreman says, "You must have an intelligence test". The Irishman said, "Alright." So the foreman says, "What is the difference between joist and girder?". And the Irishman said, "Joyce wrote *Ulysses* and

Goethe wrote *Faust*." '

In Australians' eyes, his comedy act hadn't altered greatly; he still retailed his enduring stories of heaven, hell, and the sins of the flesh sprinkled with more topical yarns about nuclear war, sperm donation and AIDS. To the gossip columnists, he was still an enigma. When they tried to get him to talk about his divorce, and his former wife, Judith Stott, his smile vanished as he bluntly told them. 'I have nothing to say about that'. Few of them dared persevere with their questions. Even those Australians who felt they knew Dave Allen had to admit that there was still an aura of mystery about the man, doors they had no keys to. In his travels, he seemed a loner, even when pictured in the company of pretty women in hotel foyers or at public receptions.

Yet, his affection for Australia and its people had by no means waned. He felt indebted to the country for providing him with a start in television, for opening the door to success in Britain. He saw it as a friendly, open society with a great heart that had never failed to extend him a warm welcome. 'I cannot stay away,' he once said to an old friend in Melbourne, 'I feel I must keep coming back'. Despite his fairly regular visits, the press never once ignored him, and it was this faith in him that was most reassuring. There was also the realization that his popularity had not diminished, a fact highlighted by his current tour. He told himself, as he left Australia that spring, that if, and when, he retired from the business he would miss more than anything else playing to audiences in Sydney, Melbourne and Perth. When someone suggested he retire there, paint for a living, he smiled whimsically as he said, 'Maybe ... but I never plan ahead ...'

After Australia, it was two nights with *An Evening with Dave Allen* in Los Angeles, then he moved on again to Canada. He had become a wanderer and the funny thing was that he found no difference in the response by audiences – they more or less laughed at the same jokes. He was intrigued by new places, new people. He noticed things and he noticed his own reaction to things. Parks, for instance fascinated him. 'I'll walk into a park and I'll read the byelaws they have posted there – something you never do normally. If you really read the byelaws, you'd never go into the park, so many things are forbidden. For instance, you can't land in a helicopter in the park or, if you can, you can land it only on a certain spot. But who would want to land a helicopter in the park?'

In Los Angeles, they tended to find a rigidity about Allen, underneath the amiable manner. In other places they called it 'depth' and not everyone could fathom him; it was not so much that he was wearing a mask, rather his tendency to hold something back. There grew up misconceptions about him, but he did not wish to clear them up. As he explained to Mike Bygrave in the *Mail on Sunday*, 'No, because that would mean talking about my private life which I'm not about to do.'

However, the one misconception he did agree to correct concerned his brother John, who had died tragically. Press reports suggested John was a failed comedian, but Allen explained, 'I don't think it ever entered his head to make a career as a comic. He was a different man from me altogether, though we were very close.' In Los Angeles, they were curious why he had neglected movies, nor lived in Hollywood, but he tended to describe himself as lazy and a procrastinator, uninterested in extending his talents into longer forms, such as a play or novel. He explained that he was not a writer in the practical sense of sitting down and doing it over a period of time. He preferred to work things out of his head. He liked to sit down and read and think. Yet, he felt he knew the loneliness of the long-distance writer – and comedian.

Allen saw comics as insular people, because they had to be. They had to spend a lot of their time on their own, to get to know what their comedy was and how to present it. As he said, 'You are presenting a part of you, you're not just doing gags.' Before a performance he sat at home or in his hotel reading and thinking and listening to music. He might draw inspiration from reading some heavyweight reports on recent medical advances in transplants and the treatment of stress. So engrossed could he become that one American journalist asked him had he ever thought of becoming a doctor. 'No,' replied the comedian, 'it is the raw material for my shows'. The journalist decided he was 'the thinking man's comic'.

Back in England that autumn 1989 his mind began to revert to television, but he felt unsure as he relaxed at his Kensington home. He was weary after his extended travels and knew he must be reinvigorated before he could contemplate any new TV series. For relaxation, he played music, painted and read books. He felt his best TV work had been done for BBC. For example, when he made a brief foray into ITV it ended without a show being produced and ITV resisting his perfectionism. He saw his TV work as 'fairly precise', and explained, 'I mean, if I'm doing a sketch about King John, I want it to be the real King John, not some cod, jokey version. That means rehearsal and production values which are expansive.'

For the comedian, ITV lacked this kind of precise approach.

22　A Stormy Comeback

For four years, his mischievous smile had been missing from the screen, suggesting that his love affair with television was over. So, when it was announced that he would make his comeback in a six-part comedy series for BBC1 in January of 1990, there was understandable surprise. At fifty-three, Allen was grey-haired and avuncular and made no secret that he was looking forward keenly to the challenge. Friends who enthused about his comeback were told however by the comedian, 'I still am retired, but in order to keep myself in retirement in the manner in which I'm accustomed, I have to work. It's an Irish retirement.'

There were other reasons. The corporation's faith in him was reassuring, and the series aimed at adult viewers would be screened at ten o'clock. He was by now an institution, like Robin Day and David Frost, invariably a winner in any battle of ratings. His comeback prompted the newspapers to look again at his career. They made it plain he was not the favourite comedian of Mrs Whitehouse and some wondered how he had come to be known in Ireland and Australia as 'God's Own Comedian'. To the English, he continued to be 'terribly irreverent', and at times profane, though an acknowledged wizard with words.

It was noticeable that he still guarded his private life like a jealous husband his flighty young wife. He tended to bore columnists by telling them that his private life was his own, so that whenever they went along to his house in Kensington to interview him they came away with little new, except a repeat of his life style, his latest paintings, his love of cooking, and his awareness of his own mortality. He was not reluctant to talk about his children: Jonathan, his stepson, was in the world of computers, his daughter Jane in the technical side of the theatre, and his son Edward was at university. He remembered with deep sadness his own brother John and the waste his untimely death had been. 'Such a waste,' he'd say in a whisper. 'My brother was a charming, delightful character. And now, when I walk around, I see the *real* him, the young, the optimistic, the wild side.'

They had both begun as aspiring comedians together, and now Allen, thirty-three years on, was modest about his own success, unwilling to over-capitalize on what he had achieved. He admitted there were pressures and it was one of the reasons why he had bought his 'retreat' in Kensington; he saw it as *the* escape. However, he was never the one to shirk hard work and once more he approached his new TV series with the enthusiasm of a beginner, seeing to every small detail, ensuring that every punchline struck home.

The first show in the series *Dave Allen* was scheduled for Saturday 6 January. It had been recorded and edited down to thirty minutes. Everything had proceeded in the smooth and funny Allen style until the comedian came to the last joke, which ran, 'We spend our lives on the run: We get up by the clock, go to work by the clock, eat and sleep by the clock, get up again, go to work – and then we retire. And what do they give us? A f ... ing clock.'

Hardly had the show ended, when the complaints began to flood into the BBC. Viewers said they were shocked by the coarseness of the language, others called for a BBC apology. Soon the corporation realized it was no ordinary protest, that the complaints were nation-wide. A spokesman stated, 'We have received a number of complaints. But we always think carefully about the use of strong language. The context of the humour, and the show's scheduling at ten o'clock were factors in the decision to screen it. Dave Allen's humour is designed for grown-ups and is well known for its cutting edge.'

Later, when papers contacted the comedian at his

home, he sounded angry as he told them, 'I have no comment to make. We could stand here all night and I wouldn't tell you anything.' Next day the papers reminded their readers that it wasn't the first time the comedian had been in hot water; there was the Dudley Moore and Peter Cook episode in Sydney, when Allen hosted a TV chat-show and words like 'masturbation' and 'homosexuality' were bandied about; in 1975 he annoyed a tiny minority of viewers in Britain with a sketch that showed the Pope doing a striptease; while in 1984 Mary Whitehouse had objected to a humorous account of a post-coital conversation between two lovers. The reality was of course that he had been seldom out of the headlines, so few people could have been less surprised than Allen himself at the orchestrated outrage that now greeted his use of the word 'f ... ing'.

Nevertheless, the storm continued to blow around him. Monday's papers were full of his name. Tory MP Robert Hayward said he intended protesting in Parliament, and claimed that Allen went through 'the full gamut of Anglo-Saxon swear words' in his BBC 1 programme on the previous Saturday night. And he added,

> Speaking as a regular rugby football referee, I can say that this was worse than anything I have ever heard on the field of play. It was the language no man would use in front of a female. And although it was screened after nine o'clock at night, it was immediately before the football highlights which, no doubt, many children were waiting to see.

By now, the row was in danger of becoming a political football. Other MPs joined in the criticism. Tory Ivan Lawrence, chairman of the backbench home affairs committee, said, 'The BBC ought not to be allowed to get away with something that will obviously upset a lot of viewers.' Toby Jessel, Conservative MP for Twickenham, demanded greater control over programmes by the BBC. 'It is in poor taste', he added. However, as though to put the whole matter in perspective, Tory Sir John Wheeler, chairman of the Commons select committee on home affairs, accused Allen's critics of 'prudism and bigotry'. 'It's the sort of language you will hear if you go to your local pub,' he said, 'or in many other areas of life. People don't have to watch Dave Allen, who is known to be a *risqué* entertainer, if they don't want to.

The *Daily Mail* took the unusual step of asking its theatre critic Jack Tinker to comment on the *cause célèbre*. Normally, its TV critic would be given the task of commenting on such issues. Tinker made his position clear from the outset,

> Before Mrs Whitehouse and the rest of her clamorous crew on the battleship *Close Mind* imagine that they have signed on a new recruit, let me say I was not shocked by Mr Allen's profanity, though I'm sure there are many who were. I was just depressed. Depressed that it should be a comedian of Dave Allen's high calibre who offers us one more example of Prince Charles's lament against our rapid descent into what he vividly described recently as a dismal wasteland of barbaric cliché and casual obscenity.

In Tinker's view, the comedian's vision of life was abrasive, challenging and at times downright disturbing. That wry smile, the roguish twinkle and the Irish charm were simply the comic disguise he used to duck through our defences. Dealing with the current rumpus, the critic observed, 'But what a silly, lazy way for Mr Allen to rouse up a public furore. What a moronic act for such an intelligent man to stoop to on prime time television.'

On Tuesday 9 January, the BBC issued an apology. The corporation admitted that a warning should have gone out before the show, telling viewers some of the language might cause offence. It hadn't happened and on reflection that was a matter of regret. James Moir, head of BBC TV light entertainment which produced the show was speaking on BBC TV's *Open Air* programme. He said, 'On those occasions when *this* word has been used in the past on BBC Television, the programme has normally been preceded by a warning. It didn't happen on this occasion and we are sorry.'

At his home in Kensington the comedian was unrepentant, if not downright annoyed by the furore. He exhibited no sense of guilt, instead tried to justify the use of *that* offensive word. As he explained,

> I mean, 'blooming clock' wouldn't have worked, 'bloody clock' would have been only half as funny. We might as well invent a new word, glug, that you must not say. You send around an edict to publishers and broadcasters that the word glug is banned. And then I'd say, 'They give you a glugging clock', and people would shriek, 'He said glug. How dare he say glug in front of the children who might be waiting up for the football.'

While the BBC assured viewers that the series would continue, it emphasized that for the rest of the five shows full public warnings would be given if material liable to give offence was contained in them. But they would make no cuts in the shows despite the controversy that had arisen. Anyway, the programmes had already been recorded. The BBC spokesman added, 'We do not apologize for Mr Allen. If we were worried about his language, we would not have employed him in the first place.'

Most of the newspapers saw the episode as a storm in a teacup, and this was underlined in Peter Tory's summing up in his piece in the *Daily Express*,

> Allen's humour is grown-up, after dinner humour. It is the kind of humour exactly right for ten onwards on Saturday night, to be enjoyed by a mixed, worldly group of close friends, bad words, irreverent religious jokes, sex, but packaged in wit. The whingers complain that Allen debases himself with vulgarity. Nonsense.

If it had been the comedian's avowed aim to win quick publicity, it had worked like a charm. Everybody, or so it seemed at the time, was talking about the new series. But in the welter of words the real issue got blurred. The question of taste and sensitivity seemed to be overlooked, in fact few papers accused the comedian of actually indulging in a tasteless joke, one that undoubtedly left a bad taste in the mouths of many viewers. Like a true

Irishman, Allen had an answer for everything. He was
determined to defend his own position and denied that it
was an act of desperation. He accepted invitations to
lunches with reputable journalists to hammer home his
case to them. They listened, heeded what he said, yet few
papers proffered their own views.

To Anne Caborn of the *Guardian*, he reasoned in
persuasive words, 'Language is there to be used. If you
sanitize it you have taken everything out of it. You end up
taking good words out of, like rebellion, revulsion, or kill,
or die, or bomb. You get somebody like President Bush
talking about "doo-doo". What are we really talking about
then?' He said that the point in question on the Saturday
night show was how we all live our lives by the clock; we
get up, we go to work, we came home, our existence
compartmentalized by seconds, minutes, hours, until we
finally retired. Then, traditionally, we were given a clock.
"It's a disdainful word because it's not a damn clock, it's
not a silly clock, it's not a doo-doo clock, it's a f ... ing
clock.".'

He recalled his appearance on the Ed Sullivan show
years before, when a joke about an Irish funeral was cut
because he used the word lavatory. 'They asked me if I
could change it to men's room. I ask you.' Except for the
fact that expletives had replaced lavatories at the hub of
the controversy, Allen thought that TV comedy had
regressed rather than progressed. As though to suggest
that he was a pacemaker, he added, 'I'm not the judge and
jury, but there is a blandness. It's not confined to Britain,
it's throughout the world and it's to do with economics.
Television, in most cases, is not made up of developers or
creative minds – it's made up of accountants and the
bottom line. It's all grey people.'

Miss Caborn, like other journalists, found it difficult to
stop the comedian when in full flight or when he began to
generalize. The argument that television must be
tempered to protect the viewer, particularly the younger
viewer, carried little weight, she noted, with him. He went
to pains to explain:

I don't sit down and analyse television, but basically, I watch what I want to watch. That's always been the criterion for me and my children. The trouble is that the meaning gets lost. People hear a swear word, a curse, bad language – they don't actually hear what you're saying.

More insidious, in his view, was the use of the twee euphemism and a form of sexual innuendo that had its roots in the school playground and pre-pubescent bike-shed humour. Just when Miss Caborn tried again to get in a word, the comedian went on:

There are too many double standards. It would be so easy to put in a bleep and people would laugh at the bleep. The bleep is used on very early evening television and people think 'Oh, gosh, aren't we being naughty?' It's like kids in the corner saying tits and nipples and willies. It's one of those things I don't like about British humour, the nudge-nudge and the knickers and the description of breasts and boobs. If I were a woman I'd be very angry about comedy over the years, because it makes things tacky.

The idea that it's all right to talk about big boobs and use humour against homosexuals is very tiny-minded. Instead of broadening your mind it closes it. You end up with stereotypes – all Irish are thick, all Jews are mean, all Frenchmen are lascivious.

To journalists, the comedian invariably sounded convincing, a kind of poor man's philosopher, an observer of the human condition above the ordinary. He had already made a sound case, in his own view, for including *that* word in his programme. He was still defiant and said he regarded the whole controversy as 'a little storm'. He assured Miss Caborn over a hearty luncheon that he had no intention of removing certain words from his programmes. As he emphasized,

If they suddenly say 'You have to cut those words out, or you have to go through and see what you've said', then you've given in. You've not given in to the eight or nine or

twelve million people who have watched the show; you've
given in to the complainers.

This is a little storm, but it will frighten a lot of people, a
lot of producers, directors, programme-makers, because in
many ways it acts as a block. It's not quite burning books
but it's the same type of thing.

It was too early as yet to say whether it would frighten
producers and thus set a guideline; it was true, however,
that the BBC had seriously underestimated its viewers'
sensitivity, and, on its own admission, was determined
that the liberty taken by Allen would in future be the
exception rather than the rule. Other comedians were
expected to take note. To Miss Caborn, the comedian was
simply not prepared to eat his words, although he had put
away in style the meal, comprising a little smoked salmon,
grilled Dover sole off the bone, a green salad, and a brown
bread roll with a little butter.

Inevitably, the Sunday papers latched on to the
'outrage' as the tabloids liked to call Allen's slip from good
taste. In the *Sunday Times* Valerie Grove profiled the
comedian and recognized his genius to hold audiences
just by spinning a random observation ('Skin. Skin is very
interesting ...') into a monologue. He did not tell gags; he
reflected on life. Life contained the odd forbidden word,
and last week *that* word landed him in trouble.

Miss Grove found the comedian 'surprised but not
contrite'. He had recorded an hour, carefully edited down
to half. The BBC, he said, hadn't even discussed the
offending word, on a show going out at the post-curfew
time of ten o'clock. He insisted once more that no other
word would have fitted the punchline. And calmly added,
'I've been performing on TV for twenty-five years. People
know what I'm about. They know what I am and what I
do. If people are going to be startled by me, they don't
watch.'

He reminded Miss Grove that he had been in trouble
before. As he recalled, 'I've been in trouble for talking
about mortuaries, or Harold Wilson. Every subject has its
followers, who feel offended on behalf of someone else.

But I've seldom had anything but praise from priests, nuns, vicars, rabbis. There is a great folly in allowing anything to become sacrosanct that there can be no humour about it.'

To some people, his argument appeared to be sidetracking the cause of the 'outrage' which was simply the use of the Anglo-Saxon word. It wasn't about sending up sacrosanct institutions or mocking nuns or masturbators – it was more fundamental. In the eyes of some people, the comedian's reputation had been damaged by the controversy. What used to be fun for them was now vulgarity. And his 'new' standing seemed to be reflected in a challenge by fellow comic Bernard Manning, who was no angel himself in the blue jokes league.

From Manchester, where he was appearing in cabaret, Manning called on the BBC to drop its blue joke ban, and claimed that Allen was getting away with 'blue murder'. He challenged his fellow comedian to a four-letter word TV contest, and said no one in the business was funnier than Bernard Manning. He wanted the BBC to screen a late-night blue gag show. 'If the BBC is letting Dave Allen tell blue gags and use foul language, why not open it up to other comics and make it really funny?'

In a funny sort of way, the boisterous Manning had a point. If one comedian could gain notoriety by using *that* word on TV why couldn't others? Manning assured the world that he was serious about the challenge, though he was more determined to make his point. At his home in Kensington, Allen remained silent about the challenge, believing by now that the storm had died down and that in his interviews to the posher newspapers he had justified his use of the word. To the majority he obviously remained what the Irish liked to call 'a charmer', but in the business itself there was at least one celebrity who had his own opinion of the Dave Allen Saturday night comedy series.

That spring of 1990, Ernest Maxin was directing a new West End musical, *Bernadette*, at the Dominion Theatre. For a man accustomed to spectacular TV successes with stars like Jack Benny, Petula Clarke, Nana Mouskouri, Marlene Dietrich and Dave Allen, it wasn't a particularly auspicious occasion. Reviews were mixed and with poor attendances the show came off early. The musical was something Maxin wanted to do and he had no regrets. The heading in the *Daily Telegraph*. 'WAITING FOR A MIRACLE' summed up the general view of this musical based on the Miracle of Lourdes. Outside theatre, he was now a freelance director operating successfully in Britain and Germany. When Allen's name came up in conversation, he said he was hoping one day to cast him in a television thriller. 'I've always admired Dave's acting ability and for years I've wanted him for a thriller part. I hope he can find the time.'

Earlier in the year, he had watched the comedian on his comeback with the BBC and was dismayed by what he heard on the first programme of the series. Up to the last joke about the clock, Maxin regarded his performance as impeccable as ever, his charm undeniable and he felt the comedian had no need to resort to coarse language to get a punchline across. 'Dave could have suggested the word and I think he would have got an even bigger laugh. Did he overrule his producer? I would think not. He is a practical man and in my view if his producer pointed out to him that something was in bad taste he'd listen. In this case, I don't think the question of using *that* word was raised.'

Maxin was convinced that Allen did not have to use crude language to get laughs; he was remarkably funny anyway. 'I do hope,' he argued, 'that Dave doesn't become misled by all this crudity that is around us today. Bob Hope and Jack Benny avoided it and still got plenty of laughs. Furthermore I find some of the alternative comedy around quite insulting and again I hope Dave avoids that track.'

None the less, Maxin continued to admire Allen's depth as a comic artist, his unique perception and his supreme art of story-telling. As he said,

> Dave is ahead of other comedians; he knows what is happening in the world outside and he tends to use everyday events in his stage and TV humour. Inside, he is

an emotional man, very sensitive and gentle. He does not like to show people he is emotional and prefers instead to keep that emotion for his performances. In my book, he is the most perceptive comic around, has been for years.

At his lovely bungalow in Brockenhurst where he lived in retirement with his wife Daphne, producer Peter Whitmore, who had made his name working on the series, *Dave Allen at Large*, remained a good friend of the comedian, and refused to be drawn on the BBC controversy. He preferred to remember their days together on the series, when they travelled from London to Brockenhurst to shoot some scenes for the sketches. The Whitmore bungalow was situated directly opposite the expansive greenery and wood where they used to shoot the Robin Hood sketches. 'Dave called in to see me once on his way to London', Whitmore recalled. 'He is as chirpy as ever and great company. He joined my wife Daphne and myself for lunch and we spent the time talking about the past and not the present. With his newfound love of painting I cannot say whether he now wants to make people laugh. Yet, I agree, he is too young to retire.'

In Norwich, Dick Condon who had moved on from his successful management of the Theatre Royal, thought that Dave Allen had been guilty of a 'mental aberration' in his January programme when he upset some viewers, and he could not see a recurrence. 'I haven't changed my views about Dave's brilliance as a comic', he said. 'And I'm sure others haven't. He was telling that story about the clock and actually he couldn't resist using *that* word. I can understand, and I do hope others will not condemn him for it. The truth is, Dave uses words as other people use toothpaste.'

Back in Dublin, where he has many admirers, the controversy had been followed with burning interest. He was condemned out of hand by the sanctimonious and the more prudish elements in Irish society, and labelled for the first time, 'The Devil's Own Comedian.' However, the majority of Dubliners continued to call him, 'God's Own

Comedian', and as regular confession-goers they asked the Lord to forgive him his *sin* and prayed that he would never again use that *effing* word.

As time passed however it became apparent that in the eyes of others he was a blue comedian and they took a censorious view. He had done the unforgivable – he had embarrassed them in their own sitting-rooms, shocked them without warning. At that moment, his stature as a comedian had diminished, in their eyes he was no longer funny, he had broken a confidence, he could no longer be trusted. Coming from 'one of their own' it seemed all the more hurtful, as if Ken Dodd in the middle of his hilarious stage show in the Grand Theatre, Blackpool, had sworn at his friendly audience and used *that* word for maximum affect. Undeniably it was both sad and absurd that Allen had alienated so many people by a single television performance; it was a cruel fate to befall any funny man, particularly a man like Allen who prided himself in knowing his audience as well as he knew the human condition.

All the time he remained unrepentant, hidden snugly away like a monk in his Kensington home. Yet he never brooded, refused to see himself as the guilty one, and continued to spend hours painting, reading, playing music, all the time blissfully unaware of the changed attitude towards him.

Now in semi-retirement, Allen preferred not to think of people, it was enough that for thirty years he had made them laugh at the absurd and ridiculous. If asked about the TV show in question, all he'd say was, 'Didn't they know what to expect from me?' He had no regrets. If some people wanted to see him as a blue comic, that was their business. Ever the traveller, he was off again to New Zealand in late 1990, hoping also to take in Australia. Along the way he would write new jokes and stories. The thought of real retirement had not as yet entered his restless mind. 'I keep in touch with the world', he would say, and for Allen that meant socially, politically and artistically. And, as always, he refused to plan for the future. He felt happier that way. He was fulfilled.

Epilogue

By January 1991, Allen had, it seemed, gone into self-imposed hibernation, content to cut the lawn in his Kensington home, travel occasionally to his remote cottage in Connemara, or even grow old gracefully. It wasn't true. His mind was busy on ten topics which he had been working on and thinking out for months. Topics like sex, the battles between humans and modern technology, politics and children's demands. As he wandered around, incognito, he observed others and their habits. He remained a very conscious student of humanity.

After nearly five years absence from the West End stage, he was about to make a comeback. Because of his self-imposed silence, people could be excused for forgetting about him, yet when his show, *Dave Allen*, was announced for the Strand Theatre, interest was instantly revived. The comedian's press agent was inundated with enquiries for interviews. Predictably, Allen revealed only as much as he wanted to reveal about himself and his private life. He shared his large house with his girlfriend, his children were grown up and gone, and that was that. He could not see why anyone would want to learn more. Most of the journalists who talked to him at his home or in restaurants were satisfied with the crumbs of information and filled out their pieces with stories of his childhood days in Dublin, his years in Australia, and his television successes. There was not a whiff of scandal to meet the demands of the Sunday tabloids.

To some columnists, he was a mystery, for all he did was chat on stage. No supporting acts. No gorgeous girls to give the ageing comedian a respite. As always, he was polite in conversation, affable in manner. 'Dave's a likeable Irish bloke', summed up one young journalist. Allen admitted that he greatly admired Alastair Sim because he never gave an interview, but he could not see himself emulating Sim. He talked about his pastimes, reading, theatre shows, even the game of rugby. He tried to explain his tirades against the madness of modern life, but they were best told on the stage itself. Approaching the age of fifty-five he was conscious of the ageing process. It was rumoured that he had prepared his own obituary notice because he trusted no one else to write it accurately. True or false, it was a fascinating prospect. He did confide, though, in Stephen Pile of the *Daily Telegraph*, the lines he wanted inscribed upon his tombstone;

> Don't mourn for me now
> Don't mourn for me never
> I'm going to do nothing
> For ever and ever

To Pile, the idea of the inscription was morbid, for he believed that there was 'a lot of life left in the comedian yet'. Overall, he found it hard to be critical of Allen whose perception intrigued him, and whose occupation with time prompted him once to ask himself, 'What is the time?' Allen does not wear a watch on principle. He refused to comment on the view that he himself was the first alternative comic and spawned the present angry crop.

Tuesday 14 February was hardly the most fitting time to open in the West End. With the threat of a full-scale war in the Gulf, icy weather, and economic recession in the air, laughter seemed out of the question. However, the Strand Theatre reported 'terrific' advanced bookings. Like a clever magician, Allen pulled a surprise trick out of his bag and decided not to invite the press critics. The decision generated its own publicity.

It was not because the comedian feared the critics taking

pot-shots at him, rather that there was no need for press notices since the show was a complete sell-out. None the less, he was in his own case creating a precedent. Understandably the papers felt annoyed. One made a snide remark about Allen's management saving £5,000 by not inviting the critics. Normally there are three press nights at the Strand Theatre, with three hundred tickets issued to the press. But could the papers afford to ignore one of the most famous comedy names in the business? The answer was no. At least six newspapers decided to pay for their critics' tickets at the box-office. A few papers boycotted the show. The comedian made no comment.

The Strand Theatre can seat eleven hundred people, and on opening night every seat was taken. Anyone familiar with a Dave Allen show quickly saw that nothing had changed, for the props included only a bar stool, a drink, and a microphone. He strode on stage with a casual air, and in a soft, seductive voice proceeded to put the audience at ease. With age he remains handsome, even if the grey hairs are more prominent. He bemoaned the timing of his comeback on this 'the coldest weather in years, a recession leading to a depression and a war.' One felt for him, but the comedian has always eschewed sympathy.

He was soon into his stride, though his deceptively casual air hardly prepared newcomers to his act as to what they could expect. He began with a salvo of political jokes, one of the funniest of which was about the Saudis singing 'Onward Christian Soldiers'. He pulled a comic face as he went on to quip, 'If John Major was drowning, his whole life would pass in front of him and he wouldn't be in it.' He deftly switched to tourism. Discovering a single American in the packed audience, Allen awarded him a Purple Heart for bravery in coming to London. And: 'British Airways is offering tea with the Queen for anyone flying over here. What do you think London is? Downtown Bagdad?'

The audience rocked with laughter, but he was never one to allow them respite. He singled out target after target like a machine-gunner, aiming every punchline at the bull's eye. Hypocrisy figured high, particularly the hypocrisy of modern politicians. As usual, his timing was impeccable, his self-assurance exemplary.

The press critics who paid for their seats came away, for the most part, satisfied. Maureen Paton commented in the *Daily Express*: 'Failed journalist Dave Allen hasn't bothered to invite the critics to his show. It's selling so well he doesn't need their help. I paid for my ticket in the end – and found it good value. The old rebel-rouser is still irresistibly amusing.' In the *Mail on Sunday*, Kenneth Hurren admitted: 'Some of us were miffed by the implication that the purpose of our noble craft is to sell tickets. But Allen is entitled to his decision. As it turns out, the audience laugh for nearly three hours and rather more of his material than usual is new.'

Soon it was announced that the show's run would be extended by six weeks. With this kind of runaway success, more critics purchased tickets. James Rampton in the *Independent on Sunday* was fascinated by the comedian's style:

> Allen has been dubbed 'the first alternative comedian', but he does not deliver rat-tat-tat one-liners like his successors. His style, spun out over nearly three hours, is more saloon-bar raconteur, weaving stories into a blanket of blarney. As another well-known Irish comedian would have it, it's the way he tells 'em.'

Hardly a night passed without a well-known name in the business popping into his dressing-room after the performance. Friends from his television days, actors, comics – they congratulated him on an astonishing comeback. As always, Allen was on a high after the show, but as he sipped a glass of champagne he managed to have a word with most of his visitors. He admitted he was chuffed by the enthusiastic reviews, though he refused to comment on his refusal to issue invitation tickets to the critics. But they continued to come.

Annalena McAfee in the *Evening Standard* noted:

> Allen's a fine mimic, taking parts ranging from four-year-old girls to monosyllabic teenagers and turning anecdotes into one-man sketches. His material, despite moments where those f-words and the odd 'dickhead' are allowed to serve as punchlines, is cleverly structured and gracefully fills three hours. Allen doesn't allow the audience to lapse into complacency. We're obliged to claim hypocrisy, vanity and stupidity as our own. Some nights, he says, the rapport with the audience is a bit special. But tonight, he adds, after a significant pause, isn't one of them. 'Did you feel yourselves getting a bit smug?' he teases. No chance.

Throughout the lengthy evening, he sometimes leant reflectively on the microphone stand, relaxed and confident, as though talking to friends. A kind of saloon-bar philosopher. One of his most engaging qualities is self-deprecation, and on this occasion he brilliantly exploited it in his meditation on the humiliations of ageing. Malcolm Rutherford in the *Financial Times* chose as his own highlight of the Allen show the scene about the telephone, and to a lesser extent his observations on the fridge, as well as the constant switching of channels on the television. Rutherford wrote:

> 'The telephone', says Allen, 'has done more to damage the relationship between parents and children than anything else.' Actually, it's not just the telephone: it's also the constant switching of channels on the television, the eating direct from the fridge and the way teenagers tend to grunt rather than speak. Allen goes through all that. He claims that the children think that the fridge is self-filling. Then he switches to the child's side. 'If you fall out of that tree and break your leg, don't come running to me', he heard his mother say.

Rutherford was not the only critic to remark on some of the language used in the show. As he observed,

> Some people will object to Allen's endless and repetitive swearing, but it is an essential part of the act. It expresses the frustration of a middle-aged man trying to be civilized against the odds. Swearing apart, Allen performs with great charm, is remarkably relaxed, has a lovely voice and some splendid facial grimaces that must reach to the gallery.

Some undoubtedly found his obsession with flatulence, and his relentless repetition of the familiar Anglo-Saxon expletive offensive, yet the audience generally were far too preoccupied with laughter to protest. They identified with his dilemma in trying to retain his sanity in a world of robots, and sympathized with his frustration at the mechanization of modern life. They shared his anger at Iraq invading Kuwait, and on a lesser scale his view of banks. 'The bank does everything to inveigle my children into becoming debtors', he moaned.

Allen owed his comeback triumph more than anything else to his determination to keep abreast of the times, to bring a fresh insight into modern absurdities, to recognize the everyday battle of man against the machine and his ability to get it across superbly to his audience. Undeniably, Allen can never be written off as yesterday's comedian, never underrated, never truly forgotten. He is, as he showed at the Strand Theatre, capable of having the last laugh on his critics. And who will deny that he had the last laugh, when he decided that they must pay for the privilege of hearing his jokes and stories.' Most of them did not regret paying, yet Allen himself would have been disappointed if ignored by them. Perhaps he was having them on in his own mischievous way. The man, as everyone knows, is full of mischief and puckish humour. And he does get more Irish as he grows older. He deserves the last word: 'I remain a socialist at heart, or at least a democrat. How dare Mrs Thatcher put a gate across Downing Street? How dare she cut off a thoroughfare.' It was the old rebel talking, but he was a little premature in his outburst, for not long afterwards Mrs Thatcher was vindicated when Downing Street actually came under mortar attack from the IRA.

However, as he grows older, Allen seems to be getting more angry and anti-establishment. Ironically, it is this very anger that keeps his shows alive and topical. To the outsider, the comedian seems indestructible and can never afford to be written off.

Index